Advance Praise for

What's a Christian to Do with Harry Potter?

"*What's A Christian to Do with Harry Potter?* is an extremely helpful book for all of the folks these days who are wondering whether it is okay to love Jesus and like Harry Potter, too. Connie Neal offers much wisdom on an important subject."

—RICHARD J. MOUW
president and professor of Christian philosophy,
Fuller Theological Seminary

"Connie Neal has created an excellent resource for Christian parents, educators, and the Christian community at large. As a parent, this resource provided me both education and perspective concerning the Harry Potter phenomenon. As a ministry leader, I'm pleased to know that a practical resource is available to recommend to those trying to determine the best way to handle exposure to Harry Potter in their families."

—JILL SAVAGE
director of Hearts at Home,
author, speaker, mother of four

"I love the Harry Potter books and read them alongside my daughter. Here is an accurate evaluation of what bad can come of Harry and the good that parents can help their children harvest. Harry is now part of the culture. Learn from it and allow Connie Neal to help you and your children."

—STEPHEN ARTERBURN
founder and chairman of
New Life Clinics and Women of Faith

WHAT'S A CHRISTIAN
TO DO
WITH
HARRY
POTTER?

WHAT'S A CHRISTIAN TO DO — WITH HARRY POTTER?

CONNIE NEAL

WATERBROOK
PRESS

WHAT'S A CHRISTIAN TO DO WITH HARRY POTTER?
PUBLISHED BY WATERBROOK PRESS
2375 Telstar Drive, Suite 160
Colorado Springs, Colorado 80920
A division of Random House, Inc.

All Scripture quotations, unless otherwise indicated, are taken from the *Holy Bible, New International Version®*. NIV® Copyright © 1973, 1978, 1984 by International Bible Society. Used by permission of Zondervan Publishing House. All rights reserved. Scripture quotations marked (NLT) are taken from the *Holy Bible, New Living Translation,* copyright © 1996. Used by permission of Tyndale House Publishers, Inc., Wheaton, Illinois 60189. All rights reserved. Scripture quotations marked (NASB) are taken from the *New American Standard Bible®*. © Copyright The Lockman Foundation 1960, 1962, 1963, 1968, 1971, 1972, 1973, 1975, 1977. Used by permission. (www.Lockman.org).

Details in some anecdotes and stories have been changed to protect the identities of the persons involved.

ISBN 1-57856-471-9

Library of Congress Cataloging-in-Publication Data

Neal, Connie.
    What's a Christian to do with Harry Potter? / Connie Neal.— 1st ed.
        p. cm.
    ISBN 1-57856-471-9
        1. Christianity and other religions—New Age movement. 2. New Age
    movement—Relations—Christianity. 3. Potter, Harry (Fictitious character) I. Title.

BR128.N48 N43 2001
261.5'8—dc21   2001017537

Printed in the United States of America
2001

10 9 8 7 6 5 4 3 2

This book is dedicated to:

Casey, Taylor, and **Haley,** our three children, who made this matter to me.

Brooke Boland, who forced me to think further than I had at first and realize that Christians on both sides of this debate can be right with God, differ in their convictions, and still act with loving respect toward each other.

Linda Vulcano, who dared to listen and learn for the sake of a child she loves.

Kim Roberts, my dear friend, who asked challenging questions, supplied much-needed encouragement, and continually upheld me in prayer as I researched and wrote.

Sarah Flower, who first introduced our family to Harry Potter.

Finally, in loving memory of **Sue Flower,** whom I will always think of when I recall what Albus Dumbledore told Harry: "Love as powerful as your mother's for you leaves its own mark. Not a scar, no visible sign…to have been loved so deeply, even though the person who loved us is gone, will give us some protection forever."

TABLE OF
CONTENTS

Hear voices from both sides of the debate in their own words. What do the Harry Potter stories *actually* say about witchcraft and wizardry? Well, that depends. Is it possible that opposing answers to an important question can be equally valid and biblically viable?

Learn to tell a Gryffindor from a Slytherin, why a Snitch is good, how to pronounce Hermione, and other must-know details about the books.

Get a glimpse inside the minds of fans and foes, and consider why in the world it's relevant whether the stories qualify as classic fantasy literature.

Chapter Four

Why Kids (and Kids at Heart) *Love* Harry. 63

How These Stories Meet Specific Heartfelt Needs

Some say kids are *mesmerized, bewitched,* or held *spellbound* by Harry Potter. But there are some purely down-to-earth reasons these stories are so popular, especially with kids. Understanding these gives us important insight into kids' hearts, minds, and needs.

Chapter Five

What *Would* Jesus Do with Harry Potter? 85

Decide for Yourself

WWJD? is a personal question, and each one of us needs to be fully convinced in his or her own mind about Harry Potter. Learn biblical principles that apply to such disputable matters where spiritual and cultural issues overlap.

Chapter Six

Beware the Dangers of the Debate. 103

Subtle Snares that All Christians Need to Avoid

In our zeal against sorcery, some of us are falling into subtle snares and outright sin. Check to make sure you are not. Learn how to find common ground in Christ.

Chapter Seven

Protecting Kids from Real-World Occult. 125

Vital Information and Instruction Kids Need to Stay Safe

Regardless of our stance on Harry Potter, kids need this basic training in spiritual warfare. Written in kid-speak, this chapter will help you explain the truth about the occult and why we need to heed God's warnings.

HARRY POTTER IS HERE...AND HE'S NOT GOING AWAY!

Prepare for the Cultural and Spiritual Impact

The fact that you've picked up this book speaks to the impact the Harry Potter series has had on the Christian community. Perhaps you share some of the curiosity, confusion, fear, enthusiasm, or even anger that discussion of the books has generated. Perhaps you just want to know what all the hubbub is about. The debate over Harry Potter has caused dissension, factions, confusion, strife, and enmity within the body of Christ. This is not as the Lord would have it, even though valid concerns exist.

In the following chapters, I will help you sort out facts from fiction, reality from rumors, and provide trustworthy information to make you knowledgeable about the Harry Potter stories and the related debate. I will aim to help you become clearheaded, calm, confident, and peaceful with regard to the issues being raised about Harry Potter, whatever your personal convictions may be now or after you finish this book. I do all of this within a scriptural framework that upholds the truth of the Bible and our devotion to God's Word as the absolute standard for our lives and choices. I aim to provide all you need to obey Romans 14:5, which says, "Each one should be fully convinced in his own mind."

Why should a Christian even enter this discussion? For several reasons, but perhaps most obviously because Harry Potter's influence—on both our culture and Christian community—is truly phenomenal.

A PREDICTABLE SURGE OF CULTURAL AND SPIRITUAL INFLUENCE

Harry Potter has settled over the literary and cultural world with unprecedented coverage. No other book or series has seen such immediate publishing success (sales top forty-eight million copies sold within four years), worldwide fanfare (with editions in 110 countries and nearly forty languages), or literary acclaim (awards too numerous to mention). The series' impact has awakened a love of reading among children unparalleled in this generation. Once awakened, fans of all ages find themselves passionate about Harry Potter.

Harry Potter and his author, J. K. (Joanne) Rowling, have star status! The woman who wrote the books is arguably as popular with this generation as the Beatles were in the 1960s. Harry's face has been on the cover of *Time* magazine. Rosie O'Donnell is a huge fan. Harry has been—and is—covered in every major news magazine and respectable news venue online and around the world. When a teen accidentally bought the fourth book before the anticipated release date, she made CNN's *Headline News* and *Talkback Live*. Harry is a cultural icon able to eclipse major world events, and his influence and popularity will surge in the near future as surely as springtime turns record snowpack into rushing rivers.

Perhaps this immense popularity makes you a tad nervous. You might share the concerns of many in the Christian community over how kids might be influenced. Some ask:

- Might kids be lured unsuspectingly into occult involvement?
- Might kids come away with the belief that there is such a thing as good witchcraft?

- Might kids learn disrespect for adults and authority?
- Might kids come to believe that witches and wizards are cool, while nonwitches and nonwizards are not?
- Might kids, who make heroes of Harry and his friends, cut themselves off from the real world and begin associating with other kids who practice or celebrate the occult with disastrous results?

These concerns and controversy over Harry Potter arise along with the cultural influence and growing popularity of the stories. The debate, accusations, fears, rumors, worries, and arguments about Harry Potter have an impact all their own. Christians do not easily sidestep such discussions, nor should we. Indeed, every parent and Christian educator, and any Christian who cares about children or remaining culturally relevant, will need to face the Harry Potter phenomenon and the debate it generates. We need to do so in the right spirit, in light of God's Word, and in light of the facts, all while exercising godly wisdom and sound judgment.

Whether we like it or not, Harry Potter is here to stay. There is no such thing as untelling a story. Think about it. His stories have already entered the hearts and minds of millions of people around the world. Long before the media hype, kids were talking about Harry Potter and recommending the books to their friends. Online Harry Potter clubs and chat groups proliferate. They are some of the most popular destinations on the Web and are unifying Harry Potter fans worldwide. This bond satisfies something in the hearts and minds of those who respond to the stories with unbridled enthusiasm. There is simply no way to ignore or avoid Harry Potter's influence. The series is not a fad that will be gone by next Christmas. It is far more.

You may have noticed such enthusiasm when fans—perhaps friends or relatives—have recommended the books. Perhaps you're wondering if you should allow your children to read the books or watch the movies. In order to make responsible decisions, you need to know what is really in the stories. Besides, many Harry Potter fans are children who *love* the books and identify with the characters. You'll see them carrying the books, talking about the stories and characters, fully engaged and wearing or toting merchandise with emblems and insignias from Harry Potter's world. You may have noticed, especially if you've ever cast a wary eye or made a negative statement about Harry Potter in the presence of young fans, that kids who love Harry Potter take it personally when someone opposes these stories. They're likely to become defensive, even toward well-meaning adults. "Hate Harry Potter, hate me," they seem to say. We need to understand why they feel so passionately about these books.

If we want to have a positive influence and enter into meaningful discussions with kids who love Harry Potter, we'll do well not to show signs of ignorance about what's *really* in the books while seriously questioning or condemning them. If we take that approach, kids will write us off—especially if we haven't read a story in its entirety and have secondhand or inaccurate information. If we care about a child who is already into Harry Potter, we must realize these stories have *already* become a permanent part of that child's psyche. This is one reason we need to respond wisely rather than just react. There are many things we can do to make sure children are not misled. There are even many ways in which we can use the Harry Potter phenomenon *positively*. In coming chapters I will explain these points in depth.

The influence of Harry Potter is not only here to stay, it is also sure to grow. The series will include one book for each of Harry's seven years of education at Hogwarts School of Witchcraft and Wizardry. The first four books were out by 2000, with at least one per year scheduled in 2001, 2002, and 2003. The first movie, produced by Warner Brothers, is due out in the fall of 2001. The second movie is scheduled to be released in summer 2002, with video releases sure to follow. Over $1 billion worth of merchandising rights have been sold to date. These include video games, board games, toys, clothing, mugs, diaries, school supplies, backpacks, key rings—you name it—along with the accompanying media hype.

Noteworthy, too, is the series' growing literary and educational impact. Harry Potter has given rise to literature guides for teachers, online discussion guides, book reports, literary college classes, church discussion groups, essay contests, library and bookstore displays, research projects, and debate subjects. A literary event of this magnitude inevitably changes the cultural and educational landscape dramatically.

Short of cutting yourself and the children you care about completely off from the world, there is no escaping *some* of Harry Potter's influence. But perhaps we (and God's kingdom) are not best served by trying to escape it. Some people are reacting as if this is sure to be a destructive flood, so they opt to run for the hills. Others determine to spiritually sandbag their homes, fearing the overflow of Harry Potter's influence. As you read this book, I ask you to prayerfully consider the possibility that we might harness the cultural energy created by Harry Potter and convert it into a useful form that enlightens our kids to the dangers of *real* occult practices in our own world, while also teaching them valuable moral lessons. Not all Christians will choose to do this (and that's okay), but I'll show you how this *may* be a God-approved option for you. Whichever approach you take, you must acknowledge that Harry Potter cannot be completely ignored.

THE POLARIZATION OF VIEWPOINTS

Harry Potter and J. K. Rowling have become a flash point in the ongoing culture wars. Some Christians have brought lawsuits against their children's schools where Harry Potter is being read in class or made freely available in the library. Media attention given to the few Christians who have brought lawsuits is presented as if they represent the official position of "the Christian right." Ministers who have called for Harry Potter to be restricted from public schools on the basis of separation of church and state have asserted that the term "witchcraft"—even magic used as a literary device common to fantasy writing—is a promotion of Wicca (the religion of modern-day witchcraft). While these individuals do not represent the Christian community as a whole, their strong views have secured the attention of the secular media.

To date, this has brought swift reaction from those who believe such views threaten their dearly held rights of freedom of speech and freedom of religion. Those opposed to "Christian extremists"—who try to impose their "narrow" view of life, religion, and literature on the rest of the society—have banded together. They have created organizations to oppose those who oppose Harry Potter! Neither side is prepared to back down, because each considers the stakes too high: for one side, the spiritual safety of their children; for the other, their freedoms. In the political arena alone we can brace ourselves for a prolonged debate—if Christians are not dismissed from it altogether.

As a group, Christians are often portrayed by the media as fearful, ignorant, and completely closed-minded. The media's selective coverage of the "Christian viewpoint" in this case has failed to present an accurate perception of a diverse population of Christians. The secular media did not find it newsworthy that many highly respected Christian leaders and publications supported the Harry Potter books as literature to be applauded. Whichever position you personally hold, we Christians are all affected whenever the media portrays us—the body of Christ—inaccurately or incompletely.

Even though you may have no intention of getting into this or any other controversial debate, you may be forced to take a stand. People who love Harry Potter or who associate defending Harry Potter with defending their freedoms have heard the media reports about Christians who are trying to ban the books. People with whom you've been trying to share the love of Christ or with whom you are building relationships may begin to judge and pigeonhole you. They may negate or mistrust you because of what the media has told them you believe, particularly if they have not heard you confirm or deny it yourself.

I had such an encounter one day while walking my daughter across the school crosswalk. A teacher asked me what, as a Christian, I thought of the Harry Potter books. Before I had a chance to reply, the crossing guard interrupted us. "You're not one of *those* Christians against Harry Potter, are you?" She didn't need a stop sign; her glare alone could have brought traffic to a halt! At that moment I was glad I had already prayerfully prepared a thoughtful answer.

I hope this book will help you better understand the issues surrounding the Harry Potter debate so that you can respond in a kind and godly way—regardless of your position—if you are similarly challenged.

UNITY IN CHRIST DESPITE OUR DIFFERENCES

Our interaction with our brothers and sisters in Christ is just as important as our interaction with the world. Factious arguments have arisen within the body of Christ, sometimes causing divisions within churches, among friends, and in fellowship groups. My desire to be a peacemaker within the body of Christ prompted me to take on this challenging and controversial subject. And yet I am a realist. It seems that the debate will escalate before it is resolved, stirring up confusion that leads to endless arguments. I believe God has given me insight that can replace this confusion with clarity, for ours is not a God of confusion, but of peace. Therefore, I pray this book will be used to help each person debate in such a way that maintains peace and unity in the body of Christ as we process our personal convictions.

Even though we may disagree, Christian fans and foes of Harry Potter hold in common some concerns about the series. In the following pages I will lay out these valid issues in light of Scripture and point to simple yet effective ways in which we can address them. I understand how scary it can be to think about how the Harry Potter books are winning the hearts, minds, and allegiance of millions of children while seemingly making light of occult practices. The Harry Potter stories do present potentially confusing messages that we must clarify for kids in keeping with the Bible. Children need our help in distinguishing between the "literary magic" of a fantasy world and corresponding real-world occult practices the Bible forbids. This book will equip you to protect kids from occult influences in real life, and will help you clearly explain the realities and dangers to them. Christian parents have a unique obligation to make sure their children clearly understand what God says is off-limits in our world. Youth leaders, Sunday school teachers, educators, and other Christian leaders also need to think through the issues within their sphere of influence, while making sure not to usurp parental authority on a controversial matter of such significance. As you decide where you stand, ideally you will also better understand how others may have come to a different position and how we can all honor God in spite of those differences.

I do not write merely from an academic position, although I have striven for factual accuracy and excellent scholarship. I write as a Christian parent of three school-age children, a former youth minister (having devoted ten years of my life to the spiritual development of young people), a Bible teacher, and a volunteer youth leader. I write because I care about kids, I care about literature (having a degree in communication from Pepperdine University), and I care about the body of Christ and how we represent our Lord and his message to the world. I am mindful of the real assault of occult forces on youth today, popularized by our culture. I've fought and continue to fight this spiritual battle. But God has not given us a spirit of fear, but of power and of love and of sound judgment (see 2 Timothy 1:7).

There are many facts about issues related to Harry Potter that can be known as true or false. Whatever conclusion you reach needs to be made on the basis of truth. There is much being repeated in the Christian community about the Harry Potter books and their author that simply is not true. We should not react out of fear, but should seek the truth as we are led by God's Spirit.

I don't claim to have all the answers; indeed, I'm convinced that no one does on this issue. This is a disputable matter that Scripture says must be decided individually and conscientiously (see chapter 5). But I have learned a great deal, applying my Bible training and expertise in youth ministry to the concerns raised on behalf of kids. I hope that both the things God revealed to me through this process and the facts I carefully verified will help you and the kids you care about.

Finally, while there seems to be much unpleasantness and apprehension about these books, there are also some surprising blessings brought about by the phenomenon begun by Harry Potter. We dare not miss these! Ephesians 5:15-16 tells us, "Be very careful, then, how you live—not as unwise but as wise, making the most of every opportunity, because the days are evil." I will share with you some of the tremendous opportunities afforded Christians by the Harry Potter books and the worldwide interest they have generated.

Not every Christian who reads this book will arrive at the same conclusion. I designed it to help you come to the right decision *for you* as you seek to please God and follow the leading of the Holy Spirit in your life. In keeping with 1 Timothy 1:5, the goal of our instruction is love that comes from a pure heart, a clear conscience, and a sincere faith. Whatever decision you come to about Harry Potter, my prayer is that this book will help us all obey Ephesians 4:3: "Make every effort to keep the unity of the Spirit through the bond of peace."

CHAPTER ONE

MAD ABOUT HARRY!

Controversy in the Christian Community

Have you been caught in the middle of an argument over Harry Potter? It is decidedly uncomfortable! I raised the subject at a luncheon table during a women's retreat where I was the featured speaker. I wasn't looking to find an answer to which position was right or wrong. Instead, I wanted to see what effect the discussion would have on our Christian fellowship and unity.

At the mention of Harry Potter, there was an immediate and marked shift in the mood and body language. Ladies who had been chatting happily began to eye me warily. There was an awkward pause before one woman ventured a negative comment, recounting quotes from an e-mail she'd received from a "devoted Christian who is completely trustworthy." Others chimed in with similar opinions, nodding cautiously as those in agreement lined up verbally on one side of the argument.

I dared to ask if any of them had read the books; none had. One said she'd been given a copy, which she promptly threw away. She had read a negative article in a Christian publication whose founder she trusted. I urged them to at least keep an open mind because some of their information (cited from the e-mail) was verifiably false. They now eyed me with overt suspicion. They challenged me to prove my point. I cited research I had done in preparing to write this book and offered enough facts to deter further contradiction. I also mentioned that the same publication trusted to discredit the books had also published articles favorable to them.

My points were grudgingly accepted, but the argument was obviously not settled. The rest of the meal was thankfully short, now devoid of harmony. Ours was an uneasy truce rather than true peace. Since I was a guest among them and the speaker, courtesy required them to be polite. One woman I knew spoke to me afterward and said, "You almost lost me there. I was ready to write you off! As it appears, they all were. If you had not had facts in hand, you would have totally lost our confidence. As it was…" Her look told me what I, too, had realized. Given different circumstances, it could have gotten ugly instead of just politely cool.

Grownups aren't the only ones caught in uncomfortable situations because of the controversy in Christian circles over Harry Potter. I was at a girls' Bible club when the topic came up. One fourth-grader said, "My mom says the Harry Potter books are evil. Real Christians don't read them."

Another girl looked up sharply and rose to the challenge. "Well, then I guess that means my mom isn't a real Christian, because she read them out loud to us!"

The first girl—hands firmly on her hips—started to come back when two fast-acting moms diffused the situation.

A CATALYST FOR DISHARMONY

I don't recount these stories to start an argument, but to examine what happened *among* Christians as soon as the argument began. Arguing over Harry Potter has disrupted our fellowship and created unpleasantness and confusion. I wish these were isolated cases. Sadly, they are not. Discussion of Harry Potter seems to predictably divide Christians into pro and con factions.

Surely we don't like being caught in the middle when Christians cross swords! Even when wielding the sword of God's Word, Christians have proved cutting to fellow believers—and kids are caught in the middle of this argument. So what are we to do? Avoid Harry Potter as a topic not suitable for polite conversation? Ignore the important issues at the heart of this debate because the process is distasteful? Congregate and discuss it only with Christians who share our particular side of the argument?

I say no to all of these. Instead, we need to find a way to face the issues, deal with the disagreements with intellectual honesty, and resolve the tension in a way that restores peace to the body of Christ—without disregarding or disobeying Scripture. There is such a way, but we will never get there by quarreling. In this chapter I will examine the starkly different opinions among Christians and pave the way to understanding the complexities of this debate. With God's guidance we can attempt to resolve the dissonance—even if we don't settle the argument.

LISTEN IN ON THE DEBATE

Because the Harry Potter books raise such important issues, it has been necessary for Christians to think these through, even out loud. Those who have dared to make public statements on either side of this debate have done so with sincere conviction that their points need to be considered. For the past year and a half, I have collected everything I could find being written and published by Christians on Harry Potter. I will share some of the pro and con arguments so you can listen in. As you do, keep an eye open for the common ground we all share, such as our desire to protect all kids (and adults) from real occult involvement.

I have tried to offer a fair sampling of credible, sincere Christian voices on both sides of the debate in their own words. I have edited passages for brevity without sacrificing the essence of their positions. (Web sites listed in the notes direct you to where you can read them in their entirety.) This sampling is not meant to be exhaustive, but to let you see the stark contrast of opinions within the Christian community. I've included Christians from various strata: educators, representatives of respected Christian organizations and publications, parents, book reviewers, even kids themselves. Both sides cite Scripture, present convincing arguments, and have emotional appeal.

You will most likely agree more with one side than the other, but you'll probably also find some points on the opposite side that make you pause to think. Don't look for either side to win the argument. I'm not setting this up to lead you to conclude that one side has arguments or clout superior to the other. You will likely conclude, as I have, that there are good points made on both sides, although people tend to see it one way or the other. My goal in this chapter is not to settle the argument but to demonstrate the futility of quarreling. It's not exactly comfortable to listen to this kind of argument, even on paper. Experiencing the slight discomfort, however, may help motivate you to eagerly look for a godly way to resolve it.

From "Witches and Wizards: The Harry Potter Phenomenon" by Chuck Colson

BreakPoint—If you have a youngster between the ages of seven and 13, chances are a boy named Harry Potter has moved in with you. So have wizards and witches and dragons.

Kids can't seem to get enough of the Harry Potter books, all three of which are currently riding the *New York Times* bestseller list. But some Christian parents are wondering if Harry and his friends are suitable playmates for their kids.

Book one, *Harry Potter and the Sorcerer's Stone,* has the orphaned Harry living with cruel relatives in an English suburb. On his eleventh birthday, Harry discovers that he is a wizard, endowed with magical powers. Harry is promptly dispatched to the Hogwarts School of Witchcraft and Wizardry, where he takes classes in magic, befriends other young witches and wizards, and learns the fine points of flying on a broomstick.

In the just-published third book in the trilogy, Harry discovers that a wizard named Sirius Black has escaped from the Azkaban prison and is apparently trying to kill him.

The books are enormously inventive, and include the kind of humor that makes many parents want to borrow the books from their kids. But if you're the parent of a Harry Potter fan, you may be concerned about the elements of witchcraft in these books.

It may relieve you to know that the magic in these books is purely mechanical, as opposed to occultic. That is, Harry and his friends cast spells, read crystal balls, and turn themselves into animals—but they don't make contact with a supernatural world.

Other parents are concerned with the dark themes and violence in the books. After all, Harry's parents are murdered in book one, and throughout the books, Harry is pursued by followers of a murderous wizard named Voldemort. But as the author, J. K. Rowling, points out, "the theme running through all of these books is the fight between good and evil." The plots reinforce the theme that evil is real, and must be courageously opposed.

As this theme unfolds, so do the characters of Harry and his friends. They develop courage, loyalty, and a willingness to sacrifice for one another—even at the risk of their lives. Not bad lessons in a self-centered world.

Some Christians may try to keep their kids from reading these books, but with eight million copies of the Harry Potter books floating around American homes, it's almost inevitable that your own children or grandchildren will be exposed to them. If they do read these books, help them to see the deeper messages. Contrast the mechanical magic in the Potter books to the kind of real life witchcraft the Bible condemns—the kind that encourages involvement with supernatural evil. Help them, as well, to see how the author presents evil as evil, and good as good.

If your kids do develop a taste for Harry Potter and his wizard friends, this interest might just open them up to an appreciation for other fantasy books with a distinctly Christian worldview. When your kids finish reading Harry Potter, give them C. S. Lewis's *Narnia* books and J. R. R. Tolkien's *Lord of the Rings* trilogy.

These books also feature wizards and witches and magical potions—but in addition, they inspire the imagination within a Christian framework—and prepare the hearts of readers for the real-life story of Christ.[1]

From "Bewitched by Harry Potter" by Berit Kjos

The haunted grounds of Hogwarts may be out-of-this world, but with its blend of earthly familiarity and practical magic, it has captivated more than seven million minds. Adults and children alike have, in their imagination, followed Harry through that mystical veil between ordinary reality and occult fantasy. Most find it hard to put the book down once they start it, and when finished, may read it again and again. Immersed in this mystical world of spiritual forces, they feel Harry's struggles and share his fears. They sit with him through his classes on Potions, Spells, Transformation ("turning something into something else") and Divination, and, like him, learn some tricks of the old Craft. They sense the pain of his miserable return visits to London, and they soar with him above the earth on a magical and magnificent broomstick.

All "these things" are demonstrated in the Harry Potter books. These stories are every bit as spiritual as Christian literature, but the spiritual power they promote comes from other gods. If you treasure God's truth, may I suggest you encourage your children not to read these books? I know such parental intervention sounds grossly offensive, in fact, downright muggleish, to children who love Harry's magical world and reject biblical absolutes. Yet, just as "progressive" leaders fear the influence of biblical truth on budding world citizens, so Christian parents need to guard their children against all kinds of occult "counsel."

Shun other gods. It's tempting to believe the beckoning voices that display enticing counterfeits of all God's wonderful promises. *The power is within yourself,* they say.

Don't listen to the lies. Instead, take this sober warning to heart: "When you come into the land which the Lord your God is giving you, you shall not learn to follow the abominations of those nations. There shall not be found among you anyone who: practices witch-craft, is a soothsayer or a sorcerer, interprets omens, conjures spells, is a medium or a spiritist, calls up the dead. For all who do these things are an abomination to the Lord." (Deuteronomy18:9-12)[2]

From "Harry Dilemma" by John Andrew Murray (Focus on the Family)

From a Christian perspective, authority and supernatural power are linked.... [In Mark 2:6-12] we see a picture of the relationship between power and authority. Jesus' power flows from His authority. That's the nature of all legitimate power—it is granted and guided by authority.

When we read Rowling's series, we find that she effectively divorces power from authority. There is no sovereign person or prin-ciple governing the use of power. Magical power is gained through inheritance and learning. It is not granted by a Higher Authority, because there is no Higher Authority—at least none higher than Harry's mentor, Albus Dumbledore, and the evil Lord Voldemort.

What comes across, instead, is a kind of dualism—the idea that there are two equal, uncreated, antagonistic forces, one good and one evil, and that choosing between the two is purely a matter of personal opinion. Rowling's readers are ultimately left in a morally confused world.

In Lewis' [Chronicles of Narnia series]…power and authority are welded together. That authority is Jesus, in the character of Aslan—creator and sovereign ruler of Narnia, son of the Emperor Beyond the Sea. Good power is power that is bestowed by Aslan and exercised in accordance with his will. We see this good power at work when the children Peter, Susan, and Lucy use gifts bestowed on them by an agent of Aslan.

Evil power, on the other hand, is power that is seized or conjured—rather than bestowed—and exercised for selfish ends. Those who resist the temptation are commended, as was Digory in *The Magician's Nephew.* But those who wield it, such as Jadis, also in *The Magician's Nephew,* and the White Witch, in *The Lion, the Witch and the Wardrobe,* are eventually vanquished by Aslan.…

Rowling's work invites children to a world where witchcraft is "neutral" and where authority is determined solely by one's might or cleverness. Lewis invites them to a world where God's authority is not only recognized, but celebrated—a world that resounds with His goodness and care.[3]

From "Exploring Harry Potter's World" by Lindy Beam (Focus on the Family)

In his preface to *The Screwtape Letters,* C. S. Lewis wrote, "There are two equal and opposite errors into which our race can fall about the devils. One is to disbelieve in their existence. The other is to believe and to feel an excessive and unhealthy interest in them."

As Christians, our goal in approaching occultism should be to avoid both extremes that Lewis mentions, which he says are equally dangerous to our faith and pleasing to "the devils."

So what are Christian parents to do with *Harry Potter*? The books could be a springboard to fruitful discussion to prevent children from falling into either of these errors. But parents should evaluate the books to determine if the series is appropriate for the age and maturity of their own children. If you feel that through reading *Harry Potter* your children might develop "an excessive and unhealthy interest" in wizardry and magic, then the answer is simple: Leave the books on the shelf.

If, on the other hand, you sense that your children can grasp the deeper meaning without getting too caught up in the fantasy, and are mature enough to handle the frightening battle scenes, *Harry Potter* could be an excellent conversation starter.

If your young readers are already clamoring for Harry, take the time to read the stories with them. When references to magic, spells and divination arise, go to the Bible together to find out the truth. Help your children see that there is a real world of witchcraft that is not pleasing to God. This way you will teach your children to ask questions, find answers in Scripture and avoid the misconception that witches and wizards are merely harmless fantasy.[4]

From "Virtue on a Broomstick" by Michael G. Maudlin (*Christianity Today*)

Harry is the orphaned son of two loving parents (albeit a witch and a wizard) who were murdered by one of the best embodiments of evil in fiction that has come along in some time.... Our hero suffers ostracism from his friends.... And how does Harry cope? Yes, he gets discouraged and angry, but overall he displays courage, loyalty, compassion, joy, humility, even love.... And all the while he sounds like a typical 14-year-old. That is Rowling's triumph: creating a "cool" good kid.

What are Christians actually complaining about when they

critique Rowling? Far from frothing at the mouth, many Christian leaders have given reasoned counsel on the matter. Lindy Beam, a youth-culture analyst for *Plugged-In,* a Focus on the Family newsletter that reviews popular culture, has surveyed the Potter phenomenon and provides helpful guidance for parents. She begins by stating what should be the obvious goal for parents today but is not: "To grow kids who are wise, thoughtful, culturally literate, pure, God-fearing, and who can make a positive impact on their world."

Next she raises three issues Christian parents should grapple with before they allow Harry Potter into their child's imagination: First, the series may desensitize us to witchcraft. Second, the books don't "acknowledge any supernatural powers or moral authority at all." And third, there is "lots of gore and fright." But then she lists the books' positive values and cautions against overreaction. "Children who read about Harry will probably discover little to nothing about the true world of the occult," she writes. "We know God hates the practice of witchcraft (Deut. 18:10). But we have committed a fault of logic in saying that reading about witches and wizards *necessarily* translates into these occult practices. I would propose instead that reading *Harry Potter* produces *curiosity* and that it is what we do with that curiosity that makes all the difference."

John Andrew Murray, Beam's colleague at *Teachers in Focus,* has harsher words for Harry: "By disassociating magic and supernatural evil, it becomes possible to portray occult practices as 'good' and 'healthy,' contrary to the scriptural declaration that such practices are 'detestable to the Lord.' This, in turn, opens the door for kids to become fascinated with the supernatural while tragically failing to seek or recognize the one true source of supernatural good—namely God."

"What comes across," Murray concludes, "is a kind of dualism, the idea that there are two equal, uncreated, antagonistic forces, one good and one evil, and that choosing between the two is purely a matter of personal opinion. Rowling's readers are ultimately left in a morally confused world."

I disagree with Murray. I think good and evil are clear and absolute in the books, just not fully explained—yet. It may be your "personal opinion" that it is right to serve Lord Voldemort, but every reader knows which side you have chosen. And I would shout a little more loudly the wonderful virtues that are modeled in the books, which is why Charles Colson and Fuller Seminary president Richard Mouw have reviewed the books positively.

Still none of the critics sounds like a simplistic book-burner to me. We may disagree on details, but we share the same concern in taking seriously our charge to raise morally and religiously informed children. Overall I think the Christian community can feel proud of how it has mobilized itself regarding Harry.

To be sure, the ending is scary, which often happens when one tries to portray true evil, and so several reviewers suggest the books be limited to children ten and older, which sounds right to me. Yet as the book closes, Harry's future looks promising and intriguing: Harry has grown up and become a true player in the moral battle of his time, in a world where many witches and wizards do not want to admit there is a war.

For the Christian readers, this and other themes in this non-Christian book will seem appropriate for the world they find themselves engaged with.[5]

From "Harry Potter's Magic" by Alan Jacobs (Wheaton College)

In the twenty-some-odd years that I have been pretty closely following trends in American publishing, no development in the industry has been nearly so inexplicable to me, nor has any development made me so happy. For I adore the Harry Potter books.

J. K. Rowling…simply has that mysterious gift, so prized among storytellers and lovers of stories but so resistant to critical explication, of world-making. It is a gift that many Christian readers tend to associate with that familiar but rather amorphous group of English Christian writers, the Inklings.

Joanne Rowling has expressed her love for the Narnia books—one of the reasons there will be, God willing, seven Harry Potter books is that there are seven volumes of Narnia stories—but as a literary artist she bears far greater resemblance to Tolkien. One of the great pleasures for the reader of her books is the wealth of details, from large to small that mark the Magic world as different from ours.

I have made my enthusiasm for these books quite evident to many friends, but some of them are dubious—indeed, deeply suspicious. These are Christian people, and they feel that books which make magic so funny and charming don't exactly support the Christian view of things. Such novels could at best encourage children to take a smilingly tolerant New Age view of witchcraft, at worst encourage the practice of witchcraft itself. Moreover, some of them note, Harry Potter is not exactly a model student: he has, as the Headmaster of Hogwarts puts it, "a certain disregard for rules," and spends a good deal of time fervently hoping not to get caught in mid-disregard.

This second matter, I think, poses no real problem. It is true that Harry is often at odds with some of his teachers, but these particular teachers are not exactly admirable figures: they themselves are often at odds with the wise, benevolent, and powerful Headmaster, Albus Dumbledore, whom they sometimes attempt to undermine or outflank. But to Dumbledore, significantly, Harry is unswervingly faithful and obedient; indeed, the climax of the second novel, *Harry Potter and the Chamber of Secrets,* turns on Harry's fidelity to Dumbledore.

In short, Rowling's moral compass throughout the three novels is sound—indeed, I would say, acute. But the matter of witchcraft remains, and it is not a matter to be trifled with. People today, and this includes many Christians, tend to hold two views about witches: first: that real witches don't exist, and second, that they aren't as bad as the evil masterminds of the Salem witch trials made them out to be. These are obviously incompatible beliefs. As C. S. Lewis has pointed out, there is no virtue in being tolerant of witches if you think that witchcraft is impossible, that is, that witches don't really exist. But if there are such things as witches, and they do indeed invoke supernatural or unnatural forces to bring harm to good people, then it would be neither wise nor good to tolerate them. So the issue is an important one, and worthy of serious reflection.

The place to begin is to invoke one of the great achievements of twentieth-century historical scholarship: the eight volumes Lynn Thorndike published between 1929 and 1941 under the collective title *A History of Magic and Experimental Science*. And it is primarily the title that I wish to reflect upon here. In the thinking of most modern people, there should be two histories here: after all, are not magic and experimental science opposites?

Is not magic governed by superstition, ignorance, and wishful thinking, while experimental science is rigorous, self-critical, and methodological? While it may be true that the two paths have diverged to the point that they no longer have any point of contact, for much of their existence—and this is Lynn Thorndike's chief point—they constituted a single path with a single history. For both magic and experimental science are means of controlling and directing our natural environment (and people insofar as they are part of that environment). C. S. Lewis has made the same assertion.

This history provides a key to understanding the role of magic in

Joanne Rowling's books, for she begins by positing a counterfactual history, a history in which magic was not a false and incompetent discipline, but rather a means of controlling the physical world at least as potent as experimental science. In Harry Potter's world, scientists think of magic in precisely the same way they do in our world, but they are wrong. The counterfactual "secondary world" that Rowling creates is one in which magic simply works, and works as reliably, in the hands of a trained wizard, as the technology that makes airplanes fly and refrigerators chill the air—those products of applied science being, by the way, sufficiently inscrutable to the people who use them that they might as well be the products of wizardry. As Arthur C. Clarke once wrote, "Any smoothly functioning technology gives the appearance of magic."

The clarity with which Rowling sees the need to choose between good and evil is admirable, but still more admirable to my mind, is her refusal to allow a simple division of parties into the Good and the Evil. Harry Potter is unquestionably a good boy, but, as I have suggested, a key component of his virtue arises from his recognition that he is not *inevitably* good.

Christians are perhaps right to be wary of an overly positive portrayal of magic, but the Harry Potter books don't do that: in them magic is often fun, often surprising and exciting, but also always potentially dangerous.[6]

From "Harry Potter: Occult Cosmology and the Corrupted Imagination" by Alison Lentini (Spiritual Counterfeits Project)

Much of the unusual power that Harry Potter exercises over children derives from a bizarre counterpoint between the most macabre and fearsome aspects of the magical realm (which Rowling describes in graphic and often horrifying detail) and the cheerful, utterly routine manner in which they are incorporated into the daily experience of young characters with whom the readers can easily identify. Just as experimental modern fictions played havoc with the reader's "perceptual frame" through disorienting manipulations of traditional storytelling conventions, so too Rowling has accomplished a Tantric-style blurring of moral and spiritual boundaries through the dovetailing of horror and humor, the seamless interweaving of the aberrant and the mundane, and sheer sensory overload. By the time a child has traversed the first 100 pages of a Harry Potter book, he or she has been offered an initiation parallel to Harry's wrought, by subtle desensitization to traditional moral distinctions, a clever bit of historical revisionism regarding witchcraft and magic, psychologically compelling story, and the power of imagination.

In the rush to embrace Harry as a hero capable of inducing a mass surrender of television remote controls and a return by children to the written word, one of the first casualties was the abandonment of a biblically informed caution about all things magical.

Magic in all ages has always represented a deep, unholy distortion of the divinely ordained relationships between creature, Creation, and Creator. Thus, we see the Holy One of Israel's "zero-tolerance" policy regarding magical practices, explicitly addressed in the giving of the law (Lev. 19:31; 20:27), in God's instructions to the children of Israel as they took possession of a land surrounded by pagan nations (Deut. 18:9-12), and in the testimonies of the prophets Isaiah, Jeremiah, and Ezekiel. Harry Potter and other stories that glorify spiritual technologies as old as sin, or find heroism in the subversive attempt to reengineer reality in the image of humanity's fallen desires, are especially dangerous to children, who feel famously disempowered in an adult-led world. Rowling's own allusion to this level of her story is illuminating: "The idea that we could have a child who escapes from the confines of the adult world and goes somewhere where he has power, both literally and metaphorically, really appealed to me." For those who seek conformity with the teachings of the Hebrew Scriptures and the New Testament, "safe magic" is wishful thinking, intellectual dishonesty, and an invitation to the spiritual deviations that the Hebrew prophets bluntly referred to as "harlotry," and the New Testament apostles forbade. As such, the "safe magic" of Harry Potter offers a message that is as morally confusing to a generation of children as the current ideology of "safe sex." [7]

From "Why We Like Harry Potter," a *Christianity Today* Editorial

It's Christmas present shopping time. Time for your 10-year-old to make his list—and for you to check it twice. But are the Harry Potter books at the top of his list—the first books topping his list for as long as you can remember—naughty or nice? These multimillion-selling stars of bestseller lists cause some anxiety for Christians since the main characters are wizards and witches.

In fact, you may have read newspaper accounts and heard radio reports of how Christians are fighting school boards over having the books in libraries. As a concerned parent, what should you do?

We think you should read the Harry Potter books to your kids.

First, we should all be suspicious of the media's hype of Christian parents objecting to the books. Reporters love the dialectic of first presenting the Christian stick-in-the-mud who objects to or is outraged by something, followed by the "reasonable" person who demonstrates how to be both moral *and* fun-loving. What remains unreported is that many Christians—such as Charles Colson and Wheaton College literature professor Alan Jacobs—enjoy and defend the Potter series.

Second, Christians should never apologize for rigorously scrutinizing what influences our children. A major scandal of our day is how seldom this happens. Modern witchcraft is indeed an ensnaring, seductive false religion that we must protect our children from.... But the literary witchcraft of the Harry Potter series has almost no resemblance to the I-am-God mumbo jumbo of Wiccan circles. Author J. K. Rowling has created a world with real good and evil, and Harry is definitely on the side of light fighting the "dark powers."

Third, and this is why we recommend the books, Rowling's series is a *Book of Virtues* with a preadolescent funny bone. Amid the laugh-out-loud scenes are wonderful examples of compassion, loyalty, courage, friendship, and even self-sacrifice. No wonder young readers want to be like these believable characters. That is a Christmas present we can be grateful for.[8]

Selected Letters from *Christianity Today*'s "Letters to the Editor"

It amazes me every time I read an article that blatantly ignores God's Word on the subject and would rather make decisions based on the so-called gray areas of influence around us. The books by J. K. Rowling I find to be offensive as they influence our children. In the article 'Parents Push for Wizard-free Reading' I was completely offended by the so claimed cult-watcher placing J. R. R. Tolkien and others as merely using fantasy to attract children. He obviously has not done his homework on Tolkien.

I have read many of Tolkien's books and it is not mere fantasy to attract, but it also leads people especially children into feeling that such activities as witchcraft are not only "okay" but can be of benefit. I know from personal experience that it is *not okay* to continue to allow our children to be influenced by the evil one and say that it's okay as long as they don't overdo it. Moderation is the devil's latest disguise for evil. Wake up! We need to teach the character of God on

God's terms and stop allowing the world to cover up evil with the disguise of moderation and fantasy.

I also noticed that in the article supporting the books there is no reference to the Bible or scripture, but simply because some see Harry as the good side of the battle against good and evil in the stories, the books are good.[9]

Phill Allen
Out of this World Ministries

An irony peculiar to the juvenile book field is that few adults—Christian or not, parents or not—will condescend to read children's books, while many of the same feel qualified to pass judgment on them.

Rowling's story, which she has described as one novel in seven parts rather than a book with six sequels, is an epic novel of good versus evil, where the heroes require help beyond natural strength, and where good wins out. Are Hogwarts's witches more sinister than Oz's? Than Mary Poppins?

It would be refreshing if Christians would look up from the pulp fiction and animated videos long enough to educate themselves in the field of literature, so they might think through and discuss its complexities and themes as ably as the world does.[10]

Marcia Hoehne
Kaukauna, Wisconsin

"Top Ten Things I Learned from the Harry Potter Books," from an Essay Contest Entry by Taylor Neal, Age 11

1. Witchcraft: Don't try this at home!
2. It's your choices that make you who you are. You may come from a bad family or a good family; but it's choices you make

that make you who YOU are. I come from a good family, but I still have to make good choices to keep it going.

3. Don't think someone is bad until you hear the whole story. You could be wrong.

4. Don't let enemies provoke you.

5. Don't judge people by their race.

6. Gossip hurts people, badly. I decided never to spread or believe gossip.

7. Lots of entertainment, little bit of money! I used to entertain myself by playing video games or watching TV. Now, I learned the joy of reading. I'm also reading Chronicles of Narnia.

8. Don't take vengeance. You may feel like it, but don't. Harry could have lost his godfather if he had given in to his feelings of vengeance against someone he *thought* betrayed his parents to Voldemort.

9. Be on guard against evil. I saw different ways evil can hide itself to look good. So, I learned to beware.

10. Choose your friends carefully. They influence which way your life goes. Pick good friends and keep them.

There was another excellent letter I would have liked to have quoted in full, but I was unable to do so because we couldn't reach the twelve-year-old boy who wrote it. It was a response to the article "Why We Like Harry Potter" posted on the *Christianity Today* Web site in December 1999. I encourage you to find his letter online. Here I can only paraphrase it. This articulate young man asserted in the strongest terms that he saw the Harry Potter books as "100%…totally…irrefutably about witchcraft…and witchcraft is a religion." Given this interpretation, he then logically concluded that the books were bad and "of the Devil." He even expressed feeling scared at the thought that a Christian site would recommend that people read witchcraft. He said he could not see Jesus recommending the Harry Potter series as good reading; therefore, he could not see how those who represent Christ could do so. From his point of view, the reasonable explanation for Christians recommending the books was that they had given in to the spirit of the Antichrist. He saw this as a compromise with the spirit of the world and called on them to draw the line (as he had) and not cross it.[11]

Are you a tad confused? The least bit uncomfortable? Did you wonder along the way if all these people are talking about the same books? Did you wonder if all these people are Christians? Indeed, they are all brothers and sisters in Christ. Although I look forward to spending eternity with them worshiping the Lord Jesus, I can't say I would enjoy being seated at a luncheon table with this group if the topic of Harry Potter came up. For as Scripture says, "Now we see but a poor reflection as in a mirror; then we shall see face to face. Now I know in part; then I shall know fully, even as I am fully known" (1 Corinthians 13:12). And while we still live in a world where we all can know only in part, I'm glad this argument has been constructed only on paper, not in person.

After going back and forth reading conflicting arguments, are you now clear on *the* Christian position on Harry Potter? I doubt it. Perhaps you're wondering how sincere Christians can make compelling arguments on opposing sides of the same issue. The duality of viewpoints and differing conclusions among Christians is at the heart of why quarreling will never settle the argument. This is not just an academic debate; it confronts us where we live and work, and it matters because it will influence people we love in important ways.

CHAPTER TWO

HARRY POTTER 101

What Are the Stories All About, Anyway?

Even if you've never read a Harry Potter book, you will find a parade of merchandise, clothing, toys, school supplies, and other articles displaying Harry Potter characters and terms, everywhere. Following is a survey of the most important characters and terms likely to become part of our kids' vernacular. These should be enough to make you conversant about Harry Potter, even if you choose not to read the books.

J. K. Rowling introduces us to Harry Potter in book one, *Harry Potter and the Sorcerer's Stone*, as "The Boy Who Lived." James and Lily Potter—a wizard and witch, graduates of Hogwarts School of Witchcraft and Wizardry—were murdered by the evil wizard Voldemort when their son, Harry, was one year old. Voldemort tried to kill Harry, too, but he succeeded only in striking the baby on the forehead with a curse. A scar in the shape of a lightning bolt remained where Harry was hit. When Voldemort failed to kill Harry, Voldemort's power was broken and his followers disbanded. Voldemort mysteriously disappeared, and the wizarding world celebrated its freedom from his reign of terror. Harry Potter became famous as the only person to survive Voldemort's curse of death.

But wise Albus Dumbledore, headmaster of Hogwarts, decided it would be best that Harry not be raised amid the adulation he would surely receive in the wizarding world. So Dumbledore left Harry with the Dursley family: Harry's Aunt Petunia, Uncle Vernon, and cousin Dudley. The

Dursleys were "the last people you'd expect to be involved in anything strange or mysterious, because they just didn't hold with such nonsense."[1] In a word, the Dursleys were Muggles ("people without a drop o' magic in them") who vowed never to let Harry know the truth about his magical heritage. They hated magic and aimed to stamp out any sign of it (including imagination) in Harry. Not all Muggles in the Harry Potter stories are bad, but the Dursleys certainly are abusive. Although they are the adults who are supposed to protect Harry, they allow Dudley to torment him unmercifully.

On Harry's eleventh birthday, he receives a letter inviting him to attend Hogwarts. The letter is delivered by Rubeus Hagrid, a kind but intimidating giant. Hagrid tells Harry about his wizard heritage, the true nature of his parents' deaths, and the source of the lightning bolt scar on his forehead: "That's what yeh get when a powerful, evil curse touches yeh." When Harry asks about Voldemort, Hagrid tells him, "Most of us reckon he's still out there somewhere but lost his powers. Too weak to carry on. 'Cause somethin' about you finished him, Harry. There was somethin' goin' on that night he hadn't counted on—*I* dunno what it was, no one does—but somethin' about you stumped him all right."[2]

Thus the mystery is stated, the battle lines between good and evil are drawn, and Harry heads off (over the Dursleys' protests) to Hogwarts to discover his heritage and destiny.

CHARACTERS AND TERMS WORTH KNOWING

Hogwarts School of Witchcraft and Wizardry: A boarding school for students ages eleven to seventeen. Hogwarts (motto: "Never Tickle a Sleeping Dragon") is an out-of-this-world place that cannot be reached apart from magical means. Students reach Hogwarts via the **Hogwarts Express,** a red passenger train that departs from Kings Cross Station, platform nine and three-quarters. At Kings Cross train station in England there is platform nine and platform ten. However, to get to platform nine and three-quarters, Hogwarts students must walk straight into the barrier between platforms nine and ten. Hogwarts is similar to C. S. Lewis's land of Narnia in that kids get there from our world, but in such a fantastic way that no child from our world would actually try to find it. As my son put it, "What kid would really try to walk through the wall at King's Cross Station to catch the Hogwarts Express?" Hogwarts is presented as a place clearly in a fantasy world that is set apart from our own. Hogwarts is a school that does not practice or teach the Dark Arts, but instead has classes that teach Defense Against the Dark Arts.

Sorting Hat: A battered old wizard's hat that breaks into poetic verse to sort incoming students into the Hogwarts houses. The first-year students sit on a stool and put on the Sorting Hat. A tear near the brim opens like a mouth to shout out which house each student will belong to for their seven years at Hogwarts.

Hogwarts houses: Hogwarts has four houses: **Gryffindor, Hufflepuff, Ravenclaw,** and **Slytherin.** Students are sorted into one of these when they arrive as first-years. Students stay in dormitories with their housemates, sit together at meals, and compete for points against the other houses throughout the school year in athletics, academics, and personal conduct to win the House Cup at the end of the year. Each house reflects the characteristics of its founder. In a song in the first book, the Sorting Hat describes the characteristics of the four houses:

Gryffindor: "Where dwell the brave at heart, their daring, nerve, and chivalry set Gryffindors apart."[3] Harry Potter belongs to Gryffindor, as do his friends Ron Weasley and Hermione Granger. Harry's parents also were Gryffindors. Its symbol is the Lion.

Hufflepuff: "Where they are just and loyal, those patient Hufflepuffs are true and unafraid of toil."[4] Its symbol is the Badger.

Ravenclaw: "If you've a ready mind, where those of wit and learning, will always find their kind."[5] Its symbol is the Eagle.

Slytherin: "Those cunning folk use any means to achieve their ends."[6] This is the house of Harry's rival classmate, **Draco Malfoy,** and Draco's bullying friends Crabbe and Goyle. Slytherin is also the house of Harry's arch-enemy Voldemort (a.k.a. "He-who-must-not-be-named"). All of the wizards who turned to the Dark Arts were in Slytherin. Its symbol is the Snake.

Quidditch: The wizarding world's favorite sport. It is played by seven players per team, who each fly on a broomstick. There are four balls in this game: two **Quaffles,** which players try to put through fifty-foot-high goals; one **Bludger,** a self-propelled ball that tries to knock players off their broomsticks; and the **Golden Snitch,** a small winged golden ball about the size of a walnut, which flies around the Quidditch stadium during the game. Each team has one player called the **Seeker,** whose aim is to find and catch the Snitch. Each Quaffle goal counts ten points, but catching the Snitch earns a team 150 points. The game ends when one of the Seekers catches the Snitch. Harry Potter is a Seeker for Gryffindor.

A FEW OF HARRY'S FELLOW CHARACTERS

Ron Weasley: Harry's best friend. Ron belongs to a large but poor wizarding family that is loving and devoted to good. Ron is the sixth son, who struggles in the shadows of his high-achieving brothers who preceded him to Hogwarts. Ron, like all the Weasleys, has red hair. He is also a very good chess player.

Hermione (pronounced her-MY-o-nee) *Granger:* Good friend of Harry and Ron. Hermione is born of Muggle parents (dentists) who are good to her. She is very smart but somewhat overly devoted to study, perhaps trying to compensate for her lack of a magical bloodline. She consistently acts as the conscience of the group and uses her superior knowledge to help her friends, proving herself to be brave and loyal.

The Weasleys: Ron's family. Parents Arthur and Molly make up for their lack of money with an abundance of love and laughter. Their two eldest boys distinguished themselves at Hogwarts before going into successful wizarding careers. One researches dragons in Romania; the other works for the wizards' bank, **Gringotts,** where the vaults are guarded by goblins. Third-born Percy Weasley prides himself on being a Prefect and eventual Head Boy for Gryffindor. Twin brothers George and Fred are consummate practical jokers who also play Quidditch for Gryffindor. Ginny is the youngest, a year behind Ron and quite infatuated with Harry.

Rubeus Hagrid: Hogwarts' groundskeeper, a kindhearted giant, former Hogwarts classmate of Harry's parents, and friendly protector of Harry. Hagrid is a lovable character with apparent weaknesses, including a fondness for drink that gets him into trouble and leaves others vulnerable, and a love for dangerous magical creatures, some of which are illegal. Hagrid is one of the few characters allowed into the Forbidden Forest, where many magical creatures roam wild.

Professor Albus Dumbledore: Hogwarts' wise and benevolent headmaster. He is the only wizard Voldemort is reported to fear, and he is one of the few unafraid to call Voldemort by his proper name. Dumbledore acts as protector, tutor, and a good role model for Harry, as well as for all Hogwarts students who seek to grow in goodness, wisdom, and resolve to fight evil.

Professor Minerva McGonogall: Hogwarts' Transfiguration teacher. She is also the strict but fair overseer of Gryffindor house.

Professor Severus Snape: Hogwarts' Potions teacher and overseer of Slytherin house. Snape seems to show favoritism to his house and shows obvious disdain and deep-seated resentment—even outright hatred—for Harry because of his past rivalry with Harry's father. Dark and shifty in appearance and attitude, Snape is a complex character who once served Voldemort but turned away from following him.

All this talk about wizards and witchcraft and dark arts is what sparks the debate surrounding the Harry Potter books. Can stories that contain such questionable elements truly be harmless? As we saw in chapter 1, Christians are in a heated argument over this tough question. Let's tackle it next.

CHAPTER THREE

CLASSIC FANTASY OR BLATANT WITCHCRAFT?

Why Christians Categorize These Books As We Do

You probably wouldn't need a book like this except that some Christians have asserted that the Harry Potter books *promote* witchcraft. In answer to such accusations, Rowling replied, "It is a fantasy world and [children] understand that completely."[1] Most parents allow their children to entertain some "magic" in fantasy stories and trust it will be understood within that context. *Time* compared the Harry Potter books with childhood classics like *The Lion, the Witch, and the Wardrobe* and J. R. R. Tolkien's *The Hobbit.* If the Harry Potter books truly qualify as the kind of children's fantasy writings the author claims them to be, some fears might be put to rest. Because we see Narnia and fairy tales as fantasy, we don't worry about a child looking for other worlds through a wardrobe, or practicing spells because Cinderella's Fairy Godmother cast a few. Therefore, the question of whether these books conform to standard forms of fantasy children's literature becomes relevant.

Even most Christian parents allow for Glenda "the Good Witch" in *The Wizard of Oz;* enchantments like those in *Beauty and the Beast,* where people are transformed into animate objects or beasts; and the use of magic wands, spells, and such—even though they would never endorse such practices in real life. In our Western culture we distinguish between magic that takes place in a fantasy setting (literary magic) and those same practices if done in a real-life setting or story. As you will see later in this chapter, your acceptance or rejection of these books as classic children's literature will have a significant impact on how you interpret them. Therefore, I have endeavored to examine and present a faithful but unbiased view of the Harry Potter books (using the first four published at the time of this writing). In an effort to help you judge for yourself how these books measure up with other children's literature, I want to illustrate my assertions with examples from familiar works in the fantasy genre.

HARRY POTTER AS FANTASY CHILDREN'S LITERATURE

Fantasy writing classically includes events and activities that could not happen in real life. A fantasy is populated with characters, objects, creatures, otherworldly beings, and animals that may be unique to the make-believe world or, if they exist in the real world, behave far differently in the fantasy world. Fantasy stories are set in a magical setting or faraway place that cannot be reached or experienced in our real world. They follow a traditional pattern that has been known to satisfy readers and listeners throughout history with elements of mythology, legends, folklore, fables, and fairy tales.

While the average reader may not recognize them, these elements are skillfully woven into the Harry Potter stories with pleasing effect. J. K. Rowling has degrees from the University of Exeter (located in Southwest England) in the classics and French. She acknowledges the influence of other writers as she was growing up. According to *Book* magazine, she "has never shied away from admitting other influences, especially C. S. Lewis. Her gift seems to be in recombining almost archetypically familiar themes with a fresh voice. Most readers after all, will easily spot other literary forerunners throughout the first three Potter books, including Lewis Carroll's Alice books, Enid Blyton's Malory Towers series, Thomas Hughes' *Tom*

Browne's School Days, the works of J. R. R. Tolkien, T. H. White's *The Sword in the Stone,* and some of the classic fairy tales by the Brothers Grimm."[2]

Let's look at the elements of traditional children's literature readily noticeable in the Harry Potter books:

Mythology

Mythology is made up of stories that reflect cultural beliefs, laden with symbolism, through which a culture tries to make sense of life, nature, and the universe. Greek and Roman mythology, for example, was closely associated with astronomy, constellations, and study of the heavens.

Mythology is full of fantastical creatures and characters with supernatural powers: Medusa (a Gorgon with snakes writhing on her head whose gaze turns people to stone), Cerberus (the three-headed dog that guards the underworld of Greek mythology), Sphinx (a monster with a lion's body and woman's head who poses riddles and kills any who do not answer correctly), phoenix (a bird that periodically burst into flames to be reborn from the ashes), unicorns, trolls, giants, centaurs, dragons, pixies, leprechauns, merpeople, naiads, dryads, werewolves, ghosts, fairies, gnomes, ghouls, witches, wizards, sorcerers, and enchanters.

Mythological creatures and characters in a story are a sure sign that it's a fantasy. Such creatures appear in children's stories and classic literature authored by Christian as well as secular writers, including C. S. Lewis (Chronicles of Narnia) and J. R. R. Tolkien (*The Hobbit* and The Lord of the Rings trilogy). For example, Bacchus (in Roman mythology, the god of wine and ecstasy) and a river god, among other mythological creatures, appear in Lewis's stories. Such usage of mythological spirit beings and characters do not necessarily imply that the author is promoting idolatry or pagan worship of nature. Neither does such usage imply condoning what these have come to mean in our world today. Bacchus came to be associated with drunkenness and debauchery, but that is not what he represents in

Lewis's story. For a more accurate interpretation, readers should consider mythological references within a story to see how its author defines them. The endurance of myths show their connection with the human spirit. *Reading the Classics with C. S. Lewis* gives this account:

> By the year 1931, Lewis came from the idea of myth as a mere false-hood to the belief that Christianity is a "true myth" verified by a historical "fact," whereas Pagan myths chiefly remain products of human imagination. Their origins are vague and mixed: "in the huge mass of mythology which has come down to us a good many different sources are mixed—true history, allegory, ritual, the human delight in story-telling, etc. But among these sources I include the supernatural, both diabolical and divine" (Religion 101). Thus Lewis comes to believe that "at its best" myth is "a real though unfocused gleam of divine truth falling on human imagination."[3]

The Harry Potter books include many mythological creatures. An enormous, vicious three-headed dog guards a trapdoor to an underground chamber at Hogwarts, but his name isn't Cerberus—it's Fluffy! Professor Dumbledore owns a phoenix named Fawkes, which cries healing tears. The Potter books also include a sphinx, unicorns, trolls, giants, centaurs, dragons, pixies, leprechauns, mer-people, werewolves, ghosts, gnomes (although not the cute little guys with pointed hats and colorful clothes we may think of), and ghouls. Alongside these familiar mythological creatures are imaginary creatures made up by Rowling, such as a hippogriff (body, hind legs, and tail of a horse, with front legs, wings, and head like a giant eagle), flobberworms, and Blast-Ended Skrewts (which look like shell-less lobsters with legs but no visible heads, smell like rotting fish, and propel themselves forward by sparks that fly out of either end).

Mythological references also abound, adding layers of meaning for those who recognize them. For example, in *Harry Potter and the Prisoner of Azkaban,* the Defense Against the Dark Arts professor is Remus J. Lupin.

In Roman mythology Romulus and Remus are twins, rescued and raised by a she-wolf. The Latin word *lupus* means wolf. Anyone who recognizes both references might not be surprised when Professor Lupin reveals his secret: He is a werewolf. In the same book, Sirius Black appears as a black dog. Sirius is also the name of the brightest star in the constellation Canis (the dog) that follows Orion (the hunter) across the heavens. These are but two of many mythological references in the series.

Legends

Legends are stories that originate with a real person or true historical event but eventually take on mythic or legendary proportions. In this altered form, elements of the story are larger than life and cannot be factually verified. Legendary tales are exaggerated and passed on in ways that fill cultural needs or aspirations. Robin Hood and King Arthur and the Knights of the Round Table are examples of British legends. Paul Bunyan and Johnny Appleseed are American legendary figures.

The Harry Potter stories use legendary allusions, like Harry being rescued from a difficult situation by the Knight Bus. You can also find legendary characters. In *Harry Potter and the Sorcerer's Stone,* Nicolas Flamel is a famous wizard known for his work in alchemy, particularly for creating the Sorcerer's Stone. Hermione finds a book that explains, "The ancient study of alchemy is concerned with making the Sorcerer's Stone, a legendary substance with astonishing powers. The stone will transform any metal into pure gold. It also produces the Elixir of Life, which will make the drinker immortal."[4] According to the Harry Potter story, Mr. Flamel is 665. His wife, Perenelle, is 658.

Nicolas Flamel was a real man who became a legendary figure. According to *Encyclopedia Britannica,* the real Nicolas Flamel was a French notary and alchemist who lived from 1330 to 1418. He was a churchgoing man who had a dream one night in which he was told he would find a mysterious book and must devote his life to understanding it. Shortly thereafter a man sold him the book he'd seen in his dream. He deciphered the mysterious writings and in 1382 claimed to have succeeded in the "Great Work" (gold making). He became rich and made donations to churches.

Scientists of the time were considered philosophers of nature. The mysterious mineral component that enabled Flamel to make gold from other base metals was called the Philosopher's Stone. Alchemists believed this to be the matter from which God formed all substances. The "elixir of life" (alcohol) was also discovered about this time.

Interest in alchemy persisted in the seventeenth century, when it divided into two sects: Alchemists wanted to pursue God's divine will as revealed in the design of the universe; materialists separated the study of matter from spiritual pursuits. Isaac Newton, according to the Biography Channel, followed in the footsteps of Flamel as an alchemist who wanted to better understand how to live in harmony with the will of God the Father. Materialists also sought the Philosopher's Stone and the elixir of life, but for wealth and immortality. Descartes, a noted materialist, said of Newton, "Though a mechanist tried and true, Newton could never be persuaded that spirit was absent from the operations of nature."[5] Alchemists closely guarded their secrets, including the Philosopher's Stone, aware of the dangers should their discovery fall into the wrong hands.

In seventeenth century Europe, Nicolas Flamel was already a legendary figure. His grave and houses had been ransacked by those greedy for gold and immortality. Legend was that Flamel and his wife had never died. So when we meet "Mr. Nicolas Flamel, noted alchemist and opera lover" in Harry Potter's story, he is the approximate age the real Nicolas Flamel would have been if the legends about him were true. Rowling beautifully applies the cautious notions of seventeenth-century "wizards"—as they were called by those who believed alchemy to be magic—to the "good wizards" of Hogwarts, who hide the Sorcerer's Stone from evil wizards who want to steal it and misuse its wealth and immortality. The casual reader need never know about the real Nicolas Flamel to enjoy the story, but the skillful use of such a legendary character displays the rich knowledge of history and literature from which the author writes. The original version is titled *Harry Potter and the Philosopher's Stone;* the American publisher changed the term to *Sorcerer's Stone.*

Folklore and Fables

Folktales are stories passed from person to person (thus the name "folk" tales) that change to accommodate the cultures into which they are passed. Fables are a kind of folktale that have the express purpose of teaching a lesson. These stories are generally intended to be scary enough, and sometimes misleading, to motivate kids to be on guard against danger and deception. *Peter and the Wolf* is a good example of a fable borne along as folklore. Often children are warned not to accept sweets, which could lure them into danger. This can be seen in Snow White (the beautiful but poisoned apple) or Hansel and Gretel (the gingerbread house). You can also see this element in *The Lion, the Witch, and the Wardrobe* when the White Witch offers Edmund Turkish Delight, an enchanted sweet that brings him under her evil control.

All the Harry Potter books carry elements of traditional folklore and fables in the plots, where the characters must be careful whom they trust, characters and circumstances are often misleading, and the villain always strikes through deceptive means. More humorous elements within the stories remind readers to be wary when offered sweets: The Weasley twins hand out Canary Creams, which cause those who eat them to burst into feathers, and Ton-Tongue Toffees. I'll let you imagine what your tongue would look like after eating one of those.

Fairy Tales

Fairy tales are fantasy stories of unknown origin. Early fairy tales, like folktales, were passed on by oral tradition. Many became standardized by the Grimm brothers, who collected and published them. Much of our children's literature has developed as variations of fairy tales. Common features of fairy tales are the use of enchantment, magic, wands, spells, incantations, potions, and other forms of "literary magic" (that is, magic that takes place in the context of a fantasy story as a literary device) used in ordinary and extraordinary settings. In fairy tales, inanimate objects become animate *(Beauty and the Beast)*, characters transfigure into animals and beasts *(The Frog Prince)*, and people interact and cooperate with animals *(Cinderella)* or otherworldly creatures. Characters often have supernatural powers, such as the ability to fly, travel through time, become invisible, pop from one place to another, and so on. While there are extraordinary goings-on, characters generally experience normal cycles of life and observe seasonal changes that are familiar to the readers. You can find most of these features in Harry Potter.

Fairy tales also often follow a traditional pattern. These elements are not found in every fairy tale, but many elements of this pattern are common to the fairy tale and fantasy genre of children's literature, including the Harry Potter stories:

The story starts in a **dismal setting** in the real world with the main character suffering, often from **injustice.** The main character may have uncaring or **abusive relatives** after the **death of parents.** You see this in *Cinderella* and, more recently, *James and the Giant Peach* by Roald Dahl. The hero is often **unaware of his true heritage.** You see this with the boy Arthur in *The Sword in the Stone* and Prince Rilian in *The Silver Chair,* where both young heroes are destined to be king, but have been deceived about their heritage to keep them from attaining power.

The main character is either **invited** or led by curiosity or destiny into a **magical world.** He or she is **magically transported,** sometimes through a magical portal. There may be a **series of passages** that make a clear distinction between the otherworldly setting and our real world. In the magical world, the main character feels **hopeful** but may **struggle with self-doubt.** The characters may use various means of **magical transportation** to get around.

The main character seeks something important or is given a **quest,** perhaps to escape dismal and oppressive conditions (as in Cinderella), to secure justice (as when Jack climbs the magic beanstalk to retrieve his father's belongings), to fulfill a need (as in Peter Pan's search for a mother for the lost boys), or to discover truth or solve a mystery (as when the children are called into Narnia to learn what happened to the seven missing lords in *The Voyage of the Dawn Treader*).

The main character discovers he or she has **special abilities** and is somehow **chosen or needed** in the magical world. Arthur discovers he is the chosen king of Britain, and Snow White finds that the seven dwarfs need her homemaking skills.

The main character must prove his or her worthiness. This may be done by passing a simple test of identity (as with the princess feeling the pea beneath a stack of mattresses), or a series of tests that require knowledge, logic, daring, courage, skill, expertise, and sometimes magic. In the course of being tested, the main character reaches **greater maturity.** He or she grows into destined goodness and greatness that was obscured at the beginning of the story.

The characters take part in a **battle between good and evil.** In the course of this battle, they face many dangers, including their greatest fears. This conflict between good and evil can take many forms, but the struggle is usually a matter of **life or death.** This is where the scenes can become violent, as in the battles in Narnia where men and beasts die gruesome deaths. Traditional fairy tales make sure that those who are good and those who are evil are distinguished by their attitudes and actions. While those on the good side are often shown to be vulnerable and prone to human frailties, which often increase the danger, they align themselves with the cause of good and are therefore victorious. When the characters on the side of good have moral lapses, they are corrected in the course of the story. In this way readers are instructed to avoid similar hard lessons in their own lives. A clear moral divide maintains that good is good and evil is evil, although evil often masquerades as good to deceive.

Evil is typically personified by a **terrible villain** determined to destroy the main character. This villain may have extraordinary skill (as with Captain Hook's swordplay) or the power of dark magic (Maleficent in *Sleeping Beauty*). Whatever form it takes, the villain must be destroyed or deprived of power for anyone to be safe.

The main character will put forth his or her best effort but can only succeed with the **help and cooperation of others.** These helpers may include other children, creatures (as in Narnia), animal friends (Cinderella's mice), or supernatural help (Sleeping Beauty's three good fairies). The hero must cooperate with those who help him, but he also has to find the courage to face the villain and conquer evil.

Finally, fairy tales have a **happy ending,** which typically comes only when the villain is conquered, wrongs are made right, secrets are revealed, and the hero has a reversal of fortunes. Pick any fairy tale; the happy ending is classic!

The Harry Potter books follow this traditional fairy-tale pattern. Harry's story begins with baby Harry being rescued after the death of his parents. He is taken to live with the Dursleys, who despise and abuse him and force him to live in the cupboard under the stairs with spiders that must be pulled from his hair each morning. Harry is unaware of his true heritage because the Dursleys have lied to him about his parents and forbid him to ask any questions.

Just before his eleventh birthday, Harry receives his invitation to Hogwarts in the form of mysterious letters, which the Dursleys go to great lengths to keep from him. Harry is astounded to find that he is famous in the wizarding world. This engages his desire to find out the truth about himself and his heritage. He is hopeful about getting away from the Dursleys' abuses and curious about his destiny and what this new world could be like, but he is also riddled with self-doubt, as any preadolescent would be before entering a new school and social situation.

Harry is magically transported from the real world to the magical world on the Hogwarts Express. He must pass through a magical portal by walking through the solid barrier between platforms nine and ten without stopping or being scared. This is obviously impossible in our world.

A series of passages make it clear that the reader has crossed over from the real world to the magical world. Once aboard the Hogwarts Express, Harry and his fellow students travel some distance. Disembarking, they are greeted by the giant Rubeus Hagrid. They see the school (a castle) across a lake. They get into small boats and glide across the lake without having to row, float through an opening in the face of a cliff, and navigate a dark tunnel until they come to a kind of underground harbor, climb a passageway in the rocks, and ascend the steps to the doors of Hogwarts.

Harry's magical world has various means of magical transportation: He travels by a flying motorcycle, flying broomsticks, floo powder (a means of traveling from one fireplace to another via the flues), a centaur, a hippogriff, the tail of a flying phoenix, a port key (an ordinary object used to transport wizards from one place to another), and by enchanted flying car. The more experienced witches and wizards can also pop from one place to another.

In every book, Harry and his friends take on a quest to rectify injustice, seek the truth, and solve a mystery, which usually involves thwarting evil schemes and saving lives.

Harry discovers a great deal about himself in the wizarding world. Not only is he famous, he also finds he has a special ability to play Quidditch (a skill he may have inherited from his father). He is hailed as the best Seeker Hogwarts has had in one hundred years.

Each story in the Harry Potter series includes many tests, including literal exams at the end of each school term, which must be prepared for with homework and intense study. Harry must face and overcome other tests to solve the mystery or thwart the evil plans of Voldemort. These require logic, daring, courage, skill, and expertise in use of magical skills. The tests are primarily fantastical, such as having to lull a three-headed dog to sleep or escape the clutches of an enchanted plant.

In the course of being tested, the main characters mature and develop. They grow in goodness. Harry and his friends occasionally falter but ultimately prove to be on the side of good. They often demonstrate self-sacrifice, such as when Ron lets himself be taken in a game of human chess so Harry and Hermione can proceed to fulfill their mission.

The central theme of every Harry Potter book is the battle between good and evil. The wizards devoted to good fight to defeat evil assaults, which are usually backed by Voldemort—the formidable villain—and his followers. Throughout the stories, Voldemort is revealed as an excellent characterization of evil: He is murderous, deceitful, self-centered, and cruel. He creates confusion, revels in injustice, spreads hatred, sows seeds of dissension, and does everything in his power to destroy those who stand for all that is good. Voldemort wants Harry dead. His power broke when he couldn't kill Harry, and he wants it back. He cannot be ignored and must be vigilantly guarded against at all times.

While in battle, Harry and his friends have to put forth their best efforts and face their greatest fears. Harry often ends up alone in a showdown with Voldemort, but he relies on the help of friends from Gryffindor—primarily Ron and Hermione—and other allies to get that far. He also relies on his teammates when he plays Quidditch, his teachers—those who can be trusted—and especially Albus Dumbledore, who is good and wise.

In each book, Rowling holds the outcome in suspense and always manages surprising and gratifying conclusions. The characters must be brave (the chief characteristic of those in Gryffindor) because the struggle between good and evil is a life or death struggle. There is always the risk that someone could be killed, because the nature of the evil one is murderous. In

Harry Potter and the Goblet of Fire, one of the characters on the good side is killed, showing how deadly serious the battle is against evil. When asked what to expect in future Harry Potter books, the author replied, "The theme running through all seven books is the fight between good and evil, and I'm afraid there will be casualties!"[6]

However, Rowling consistently resolves the conflict happily for those on the side of good, makes sure the villain is thwarted, and also ensures that even seemingly unimportant threads are woven into the whole. The Harry Potter books are a seven-year saga, so some mysteries are being revealed slowly, bit by bit, in each title. Readers can anticipate the final happy ending to culminate at the end of the seventh book.

I have just presented a clear picture of the Harry Potter stories as classic children's fantasy literature. However, not everyone sees it that way. As we are about to consider, how one "sees it" makes all the difference. It also explains the conflict over Harry Potter in the Christian community.

KAREN'S DILEMMA

Consider the plight of my friend Karen, who works for a Christian organization. Several of her close friends and coworkers are staunchly opposed to Harry Potter. When I told her I was writing this book, she replied, "I hate Harry Potter!" She gathered that I had read the books with our family, and she asked, *"How could you? How could you of all people?"*—meaning that she knew me to be a sincere Christian, devoted to the Lord, the Word of God, and my family.

So I asked her, "Do you really want to hear the answer to that question?"

She said, "Yes, I really do, because I don't understand how someone like you..."

I shared with her some of the things I will share with you later in these pages. She took particular interest in how I had shared the gospel with a family friend by using the Harry Potter story as a redemptive analogy, and how he became a Christian shortly thereafter (see chapter 11). She asked me many questions, and the answers I gave her presented a picture totally different from one presented by a mutual friend who is opposed to the books.

Karen then said something like, "I can see what you're saying, and from that viewpoint it makes sense. But I can also see it the other way too. I can agree with both of you even though your positions are opposite. But I still can't bring myself to read that stuff."

Karen and I had reached a place of understanding, although not agreement. This is a good place. It is far more comfortable than the uneasy truce reached at the lunch table at the ladies retreat.

My friend inspired me as I wrote this challenging book. She reminded me that we cannot walk away from the Harry Potter debate just because it can be confusing and uncomfortable. There must be some way to work through these perplexing issues within the body of Christ without just calling a truce. And we need to. Kids we care about have already been influenced, and we don't want to be distanced from our Christian friends and acquaintances. We need a way to understand how the same books can be viewed by God-fearing Christians in such totally different ways so we can be at peace with each other—even if we have to agree to disagree.

OUR BRAIN'S AMAZING FILING SYSTEM

Take a look at the illustration on the facing page.[7] What do you see?

I use this sometimes when I address an audience and ask them the same question. Without fail, the room breaks into confusion. Some say they see a young woman. Others say they see an older woman with her head down wearing a scarf. There is always conflict as people try to tell each other what they see. What's the key to understanding the confusion and resolving the conflict? Realizing that this line drawing can indeed be seen in two completely different ways.

I begin by tracing over the lines, pointing out how some people in our group *really do see* a young woman with her head turned away, with an air of confidence about her. Then I retrace the lines on that very same piece of paper in a different way, showing them how some in our group *really do see* a downcast old woman wearing a frown and a scarf. As people carefully focus and try to follow the lines, telling their mind that what they first saw as the old woman's downturned mouth is really the choker on the young woman's throat, something amazing begins to happen: People start to see what they previously could not, even though the other image was right in front of their eyes.

The sounds in the room change in the process. Sounds of conflict turn into the sounds of understanding and amazement. Tension gives way to laughter. Comments like, "Oh, now I *see!*" "How strange! You can see it

both ways." "Wait, I lost it. I could see the young lady a moment ago, but she changed back into the old woman!"

Those are the sounds of factions reconnecting as a unified whole.

I explain that it is possible to see the image only one way at a time, because the human brain is an associating machine. It goes to work on any unidentified data in an effort to make sense of it. Once the brain recognizes an image, it tells you what you have seen—but what you *see* is merely the interpretation that seems to make sense, considering whatever else you have filed away in your brain as reference material. Americans may look at the moon and see the man in the moon. People in Japan may look up and see a rabbit pounding rice cakes! A rabbit pounding rice cakes is there— you just have to give your mind additional information to be able to see a new image.

You can train your brain to switch from what you initially saw to the secondary image you discovered, but if you look away and look back, you will almost always see your first impression. This is because your brain made that first impression the primary file from which you view it. Our brain's ability to sort through an enormous amount of data helps us manage in a world where we are bombarded by information. Everything that comes our way gets filed somewhere depending on our first impression of it.

When you first heard of Harry Potter you probably initially filed it under one of two primary mental files. You either filed it under *witchcraft* (evil) along with things like the satanic bible, Anton Levey, Ouija boards, maybe even Eric Harris and Dylan Klebold, or you filed it under fantasy children's literature (could be good) along with *The Lion, the Witch, and the Wardrobe; The Wizard of Oz;* and maybe *The Hobbit.* Once your brain files it in a general file, it goes to work to associate it with other things there to let you know whether it fits. If the other information already in that mental file seems to make a match, you feel no dissonance. You confirm that your original assumption about where this belongs is correct. This is why you probably felt positive while reading the comments that agreed with your general disposition about Harry Potter, and at conflict when you heard arguments that challenged your mental filing system.

It takes a lot of mental energy to refile first impressions. Our minds will continually revert to that first impression, looking for additional data that supports that viewpoint. This would explain how people who initially file it under "fantasy children's literature (could be good)" go into Harry Potter looking for a funny, entertaining story with good lessons—and that's what they find—while others who initially file it under "witchcraft (evil)" go in looking for something sinister—and they, too, find what they were expecting.

I was corresponding online with a man whose first impression of Harry Potter came from an alarming e-mail full of accusations that the books were designed to lure children into Satanism. He wanted to see for himself, but first checked the dictionary to give him a reference point. In a letter he intended to send to the principal of his child's school, he noted this definition:

witch•craft \ "wich-'kraft\ noun (bef. 12c)
1 a : the use of sorcery or magic
b : communication with the devil or with a familiar spirit
2 : an irresistible influence or fascination

wiz•ard•ry noun pl wiz•ard•ries (1583)
1 : the art or practices of a wizard : SORCERY
2 a : a seemingly magical transforming power or influence <electronic
*   wizardry>*

He reported that he looked through the books and could see that "The books definitely do promote the use of sorcery, magic, and communication with the devil and familiar spirits, as well as the art and practices of sorcery with an irresistible influence or fascination."

Before sending the letter to the principal, he sought the advice of several fellow Christians: Was there any other information he should take into consideration before mailing it? In reply, I pointed out that some of the initial information he had been given was not true, and so the conclusions based on those points were therefore not sound. He and I had a positive interchange of ideas.

It was most instructive to me that this man saw in the books what he expected to see. He replied to my note with a list of questions, including this one: "Even though there are some good story lines and moral character insights woven into the stories, how can a character who is obsessed with witchcraft and sorcery, and actively communicates with strange demonic impish creatures, be a wholesome role model for our children?"

The "strange demonic impish creature" to which he referred was Dobby, a house-elf mentioned on the blurb for *Harry Potter and the Chamber of Secrets,* which says: "Just as he's packing his bags, Harry receives a warning from a strange, impish creature who says that if Harry returns to Hogwarts, disaster will strike."

Those who had filed Harry Potter under children's literature and had read this book would probably be incredulous that Dobby was called demonic. Dobby the house-elf is one of funniest characters—one most likely to make you laugh out loud—*if* you are reading the book out of the mental file marked "children's lit"! This concerned parent who initially filed Harry Potter under the mental file "witchcraft" picked up the same book and *really saw* Dobby as demonic, although there is no such reference or inference in the book.

THE SIGNIFICANCE OF HOW WE DEFINE TERMS WITHIN A STORY

However, is this an acceptable way to understand a story? Consider this important point made by C. S. Lewis on how literature is to be understood:

"Within a given story any object, person, or place is neither more nor less nor other than what that story effectively shows it to be. The ingredients of one story cannot 'be' anything in another story, for they are not in it at all."[8] Therefore, to superimpose outside, real-world definitions upon the intrinsic meanings given in the story or its context is to distort the author's meaning. Those who see the Harry Potter novels as satanic or demonic can only do so by superimposing outside definitions upon the stories. Nowhere in the stories will you find any connection with Satan. You can verify this by checking the Harry Potter books for any satanic or demonic associations—they are not in the books. Often such interpretations are not only "other" than what the story says, but are *contrary* to the meaning clearly stated in the story itself.

This technique is clearly demonstrated in an article posted on CBN.com entitled "Harry Potter: The Hero for Modern Witchcraft" by Jack Roper. The author quotes from *Harry Potter and the Chamber of Secrets* (p. 14): "The wizard family Dobby serves, sir.... Dobby is a house-elf—bound to serve one house and one family forever."

Next, the author of the article leaves Harry Potter's fantasy world, leaves the story, and finds a definition of "elf" (an assumed derivative of "house-elf") in *The Dictionary of Mysticism and the Occult* by Nevill Drury. Having noted that "Drury is an occultist," Roper reiterated Drury's definition: "Elves were spirit-creatures that were hidden from God's sight because they were unclean."[9]

Roper then makes a connection between that occult definition and Scripture, saying, "The Bible calls them demons in Mark 1:26-27." In this way he injects the occult definition of elves into a Bible verse and concludes: "Can we call these elves 'dinky demons'?"

I quickly checked those verses in Mark. They say: "The evil spirit shook the man violently and came out of him with a shriek. The people were all so amazed that they asked each other, 'What is this? A new teaching—and with authority! He even gives orders to evil spirits and they obey him.'"

Although this Bible passage says nothing about elves, the author defines the Bible term "evil spirits" using a dictionary of occult terms compiled by a self-professed occultist. To associate these with Dobby the house-elf, he actively disregards what the story effectively shows Dobby's character to be—which has nothing to do with demons, dinky or otherwise. Let's examine the logical process used to reach this conclusion:

- A house-elf appears in a fantasy story.
- A dictionary of occult terms—outside the story—defines elves as unclean spirits.
- Jesus cast out unclean spirits, also known as demons.
- Therefore, whenever we encounter elves (house-elves or otherwise) in children's literature, we are dealing with cleverly disguised "dinky demons."

Consider this: No careful reader of Harry Potter would ever come to such a conclusion by simply reading the story. No one following C. S. Lewis's guidance could come to such a conclusion. Perhaps this is what J. K. Rowling was referring to when she said, "People tend to find in books what they want to find." [10]

So the question Jack Roper raised hangs in the air: Can we call these elves "dinky demons"? Sure, you *can,* but *only* if you assign them a meaning from outside the story that contradicts the one found within the story. Common sense and commonly held dictates of literary criticism reject such a practice.

Superimposing such an external definition onto the Harry Potter books raises troubling implications for other pieces of children's literature and folklore. If this definition of elves is superimposed on Harry Potter, what are the logical implications for other fantasy references to elves? Does this mean Christians who let children watch a cartoon about Santa and his elves are exposing them to dinky demons? What of the Keebler elves who make cookies?

If one would not extend such a definition to all elves, why would anyone see fit to apply it to Harry Potter? Because their minds are actively at work trying to make the Harry Potter books fit and make sense within the mental file labeled "witchcraft," where they originally filed it. This would explain why the parent who warned about the occult dangers of Harry Potter would see Dobby as an "impish demonic creature," while those who filed Harry Potter under "children's literature" would never see it that way.

When two debaters take the same words to mean entirely different things, there is no point whatsoever in arguing—unless you just like to argue. Although people are obviously using the same words, those words *mean* something very different to each person. Such arguments will get us as far as Abbott and Costello in their comedy sketch "Who's on First?"

As long as the parties do not recognize that the same words mean different things to each of them, there is no way for such an argument to come to peaceful resolution. It will only lead to frustration and further confusion. The Harry Potter debate is problematic in this regard. Such arguments will prove futile, frustrating, and potentially damaging to the body of Christ. We need to understand this reality before we square off against other Christians who define Harry Potter's terminology with a mental file and references different from our own.

What Do the Books Actually Say About Witchcraft and Wizardry?

Well, that depends. The answer depends on whether the questioner means "real occult witchcraft in the real world" or "witchcraft and wizardry" as it is defined and set up in the fantasy world created by J. K. Rowling. Whichever primary mental file a person draws upon will have a lot to do with how he or she answers that question. I'm not trying to skirt the issue; I am trying to show you how it is truly possible for two sincere Christians, raised in the same culture, to see these books in entirely different ways and be able to back up their clear viewpoint with good, substantive arguments.

Try to see it both ways:

Emotions run so high in regard to Harry Potter that I will illustrate my point with a piece of literature that doesn't seem to set off internal alarms for most Christians: Charles Dickens's *A Christmas Carol.* Where do most people initially put that in their mental filing system? Probably somewhere like "Christmas (good)." We've grown up on that story. Ebenezer Scrooge's holiday conversion may be an integral part of what it means for you or someone you know to sense the Christmas spirit. You may even be able to recall the final lines: "And to Tiny Tim, who did *not* die, [Scrooge] became a second father from that time on. He became as good a friend, as good a master, and as good a man as the city knew; and it was always said of him that he knew how to keep Christmas well. May such good things be said of all of us! And so, as Tiny Tim observed, 'God bless us, every one!' "

Bear with me: Could God really bless such a story? Should Christians accept such a story? Let's look at this piece of literature from the point of view of someone who believes the story belongs not in the "Christmas" file, but the "witchcraft" file. What does this story suggest about the value of consulting with the dead? What does it imply about communicating with familiar spirits and astral projection?

A Christmas Carol is a story about a man visited by the spirit of his dead partner, Jacob Marley. Marley tells Scrooge that his only hope to avoid roaming the earth bound in chains for eternity is to receive three spirits. He must entertain these three spirits, for they are the only means by which he can be spared damnation. One is a spirit intimately familiar with all that has gone on in Scrooge's life, who takes him into the past. This spirit takes him flying out the window—one could argue that he leaves his body. We consult a dictionary of occult terms and see that it appears to be astral projection, an occult phenomenon where one is able to leave his body and go other places by supernatural means. Another spirit to visit Scrooge is particularly dark and shows him terrifying sights. It takes him to a graveyard, where he is horrified by the sight of his own grave.

What does *A Christmas Carol* actually say about conversing with the dead? Anyone familiar with the story would have to admit it opens with Ebenezer Scrooge having a conversation with his dead partner. But Deuteronomy 18:10-11 clearly states, "Let no one be found among you who…consults the dead." These are the same verses most often quoted to warn against Harry Potter. Isaiah 8:19 says, "Should not a people inquire of their God? Why consult the dead on behalf of the living?"

First Timothy 4:1 says, "The Spirit clearly says that in later times some will abandon the faith and follow deceiving spirits and things taught by demons." So one might rightly question a character who not only converses with the spirit of a dead man, but also welcomes three spirits in one night and somehow leaves his body by supernatural means to fly through the night with them. Just because they teach Scrooge good lessons does not mean we should accept such guidance from "deceiving spirits." They do imply that the only way for Scrooge to escape eternal punishment of being chained like his dead partner's ghost is to follow these spirits and change his ways. But Jesus said, "I am the way and the truth and the life. No one comes to the Father except through me" (John 14:6). Might these spirits be suggesting that one is saved by good works? Ephesians 2:8-9 says, "For it is by grace you have been saved, through faith—and this not from yourselves, it is the gift of God—not by works, so that no one can boast."

What does *A Christmas Carol* actually say about talking to spirits of the dead? What does it say about astral projection or leaving one's body to traverse space and time? What does it actually say about a spirit that leads one to his grave or purports that the way to escape damnation is to follow spirit guides? Even most children who are familiar with *A Christmas Carol* would answer that it does not say anything *about* these things.

Most of us, too, dismiss this entire line of reasoning. But why? Because we have already processed this story another way. We explain that these *spirits* and *supernatural powers* are merely literary devices used by the author to tell a story, not a subtle attempt to lead unsuspecting souls into occult practices. And this story doesn't even have the added buffer granted to fantasy stories where one can say the "magic" takes place in another world where such things are not occult. We believe that the story is about redemption, repentance, learning to let go of the past, and loving before it is too late. The story is good—in every sense of the word—even though it is *entirely* set within supernatural elements strictly forbidden by Scripture. Even though people today are involved in similar, dangerous occult practices, no one (that I've encountered anyway) makes this argument about *A Christmas Carol*. This is not because such lines are not sketched in the story. It is because we initially filed it under "Christmas"; therefore, we never followed that line of reasoning.

So too, where you initially file the Harry Potter stories in your mind will influence how you answer the question of what these stories say *about* witchcraft and wizardry. There is no getting around the fact that the stories unfold during Harry's seven years of wizard training at Hogwarts School of Witchcraft and Wizardry. Whether you believe the stories include occult practices will depend on whether you go outside the text to use the occultic definitions of those terms in our world, or adopt definitions given within the story in the context of fantasy children's literature.

Yes, the characters do cast spells, make potions, practice divination, and study astrology (although the last two are held in skepticism by the students and most teachers). If you are looking to find signs of "witchcraft," you'll have no trouble finding those elements in the books. But to do so can be fairly likened to finding that Ebenezer Scrooge practices communing with spirits of the dead and astral projection while entertaining doctrines of deceiving spirits. If you can see that *A Christmas Carol* is set in that liter-

ary context and also see that this is not what the story is about, you will be able to understand what some are saying about the Harry Potter books.

And vice versa.

Whichever view you take, you will run into sincere Christians who genuinely see it the other way. I believe the Lord would have the body of Christ do more than just continue to quarrel among ourselves in frustration and futility. We need to realize that this is not the kind of matter that will be settled one way or the other by arguing. Arguing among ourselves destroys our unity, creates factions, and may defeat our witness before a watching world. I discuss this problem further in chapter 6, "Beware the Dangers of Debate."

Whatever else may be ascribed to these books by the associations made in the minds of readers, the Harry Potter stories hold up as classic children's literature. They have all the standard elements and patterns that have satisfied readers and listeners throughout generations. They also have many other elements that cause children—and people of all ages—in this generation to love these stories. What warrants their passion, and why is it important for Christians to know? We'll answer these questions in the next chapter.

CHAPTER FOUR

WHY KIDS (AND KIDS AT HEART) *LOVE* HARRY

How These Stories Meet Specific Heartfelt Needs

In a cautionary e-mail warning parents about the Harry Potter series, a man who had not read any of the books but had heard negative reports wrote, "It seems that the main emphasis of the deception of the power of these books is that they engage the children who read them almost hypnotically, causing many children who have never enjoyed reading before to read more than they watch TV or play video games." This wasn't the first time I had heard such comments. It's been said that kids are *mesmerized, bewitched,* or held *spellbound* by these stories. These phrases are most often used metaphorically, but even so, some Christians have begun to wonder why kids *do* love these stories so much.

To start, the stories themselves are satisfying. They don't talk down to kids; being full of humor, interesting wordplay, suspense, surprise, laugh-out-loud fun, silliness, and lots of chocolate—all the things that make kids like any good story! But there must be more, right? These elements alone can't account for the series' amazing success.

What follows are some purely down-to-earth reasons why kids love Harry Potter. I'm not saying there are no spiritual forces at work in this phenomenon; we've discussed that concern in chapter 3. In my ministry to youth for more than a decade, I've had to confront spiritual forces of darkness. I do indeed believe we need to be alert to potential spiritual influences. However, I can also tell you that, spiritual forces aside, elements of these books have resonated with this generation. The way these stories meet heartfelt needs goes a long way toward explaining the enormous popularity of the Harry Potter books. Identifying and understanding why kids love Harry Potter will help you assess the stories. It may also help you consider ways in which you personally—and Christians as a community—can better meet the needs of this generation.

Anyone who wants to reach kids knows you've got to reach their hearts. This is the aim of people who devote their lives to youth ministry; it's also the aim of people who market goods and services to kids. Over the years, I have sought to communicate God's Word to kids in fresh and relevant ways. I've become a student of the Bible as well as a student of kids' needs and interests. In this pursuit, I read a book titled *Creating Ever-Cool: A Marketer's Guide to a Kid's Heart* by Gene Del Vecchio. His experience comes from working at Ogilvy & Mather, a company that specializes in developing brands and marketing them effectively to children. His analysis of what kids need, and respond to, heartily reveals one explanation for the success of Harry Potter. He writes:

> Children seek the social needs of love, belonging, acceptance, appreciation, and friendship. They attempt to fulfill their ego, which demands self-respect and pride. Given a child's tender years, such needs are intense, especially since children depend so much on others to fulfill them. So children strive to be independent, capable, and in control. They need to learn, aspire, and achieve. They need to dream many dreams.
>
> Through the colorful prism that is the child's heart, these needs are satisfied in many ways. And kid brands that survive decades to become phenomenal successes do so, in large part, because they found a path that satisfied one or more of those needs.[1]

Hence, successful marketers must identify and address key eternal needs. These are the needs outlined in Del Vecchio's book; they are also the needs addressed in Youth for Christ's youth evangelism training. Whether we're presenting the gospel or a new toy, the way to a kid's heart follows the paths of eternal needs. Part of J. K. Rowling's success can be traced down such paths.

By way of introduction, let me list a few of these needs that are so crucial in the lives of kids. This list is certainly not exhaustive, but as you read this chapter, you will be able to see how the Harry Potter stories speak to these specific needs:

- hope that comes in the form of wishes that might come true
- a sense of control or empowerment
- self-esteem that comes from accomplishment
- affirmation of their emotions and tools to help deal with them
- knowledge that they can face fear and conquer it
- a strong sense of identity, of belonging, and of destiny
- love that is found in loving families
- the company of good friends

Beyond these, the stories also address kids' overarching longing for the supernatural. Charles Colson, president and founder of Prison Fellowship and commentator for *Christianity Today*, writes about this in "Harry Potter and the Existence of God: Sehnsucht and the Bookstore":

BreakPoint with Chuck Colson—So what's the buzz amongst kids these days? A new video game? A spectacular movie? A hip new music CD? Not even close.

The hottest selling phenomenon of the summer is a *book*. As all of us know, it's the latest Harry Potter novel by J. K. Rowling.

It's surprising, but the Harry Potter craze is much more than a marketing phenomenon. It's more than just a popular page-turner. The fervor surrounding the Potter books is evidence of the human yearning for something beyond the mundane world of our daily experience.

In fact, you could say that Harry Potter is proof of the existence of God.

Kids were so anxious to get their hands on the recently released *Harry Potter and the Goblet of Fire* that millions of the books were pre-ordered over the Internet. Thousands of parents suspended bedtimes to take their kids to the bookstores that opened at 12:01 A.M. last Saturday to sell the book.

Not only did the book smash sales records, it sent the publisher "back to the printing press" immediately for 2 million more copies. That's in addition to the 3.8 million already distributed in this country. Gallup has found that almost a third of all parents with kids under 18 have children who've read a Harry Potter novel. And there are already plans for a film version.

What is it about Harry Potter that has kids turning off the TV and devouring books? The latest novel, while easy to read, is not an easy read: *Harry Potter and the Goblet of Fire* weighs in at over 700 pages. So much for marketing experts who tell us kids lack the attention span to read big books!

What the fascination with Harry Potter really illustrates is what C. S. Lewis meant by *Sehnsucht*—the longing for the mysterious, the wonderful, the other-worldly that our daily experience does not satisfy.

Classical Christian thinking understood that every desire has a corresponding real object. Hunger, for example, indicates that there is such a thing as food. But in our hearts there is a desire for something we will never find in the world. Blaise Pascal called it the "God-shaped" void in the human soul. Similarly, Augustine spoke of the restlessness of our hearts that could only be satisfied by God.

The appeal of other-worldly stories like Harry Potter is that they tap into our hunger for God's wonder. The banal world of video games, television, the pursuit of wealth, and other diversions can never satisfy this longing. The Potter craze reflects the longing in our kids' souls for God.

But Harry Potter is not the real thing. Which is why many Christian parents are concerned about it. Nor is it the best way to satisfy our kids' desire. But you can use the Potter craze to get kids and grandkids into something that leads them to the real thing

Take this occasion to introduce to them to C. S. Lewis's *The Chronicles of Narnia*, J. R. R. Tolkien's *Lord of the Rings*, and George MacDonald's *The Princess and the Goblin*. These books not only recognize this yearning for wonder and magic, they also reflect a well-developed understanding of the majesty and mystery of God.

If you do this—and put your kids on to stories that recognize the real thing we all yearn for—the Harry Potter phenomenon may turn out to be a pretty good thing indeed.[2]

Harry Potter Appeals to Kids' Love of Fantasy, Magic, and Wishes Coming True

"Magic, fantasy, and wishes are the staples of Children's literature because they are tried and true when it comes to satisfying a child's heart," writes Del Vecchio. "Cinderella has her fairy godmother. Aladdin has his genie. Dumbo has his magic feather. Wish upon a star and it just might come true.... Magic, fantasy, and wishes are a very important part of the Disney aura."[3]

Kids love transformation—changing in appearance or structure, or metamorphosing. In the Harry Potter books, transformation isn't just what happens to the characters as they grow up, it's also a class at Hogwarts! Some of the witches and wizards have the ability to take on the appearance of other forms, such as animals or bugs or people. Readers have to be on the alert to see if any animal, person, or thing might be someone else in an altered form. Surprising revelations come in every story.

Kids *need* this hope that comes in the form of wishes that might come true. Researchers have found that kids love to engage their imaginations with stories of wish fulfillment. And Harry Potter books give kids the kind of fantastic wish fulfillment they most often say they want. When kids are asked: "If you could have two wishes come true, what would they be?" The answers most consistently given are to be rich, to be empowered by being older or stronger, or to be famous either in professional sports or in a career. Let's look at these with regard to Harry Potter:

Kids Wish to Be Rich

Harry is kept in poverty while his guardians lavish their own spoiled son with everything on most kids' wish lists. Suddenly, Harry discovers that his parents left him piles of gold and silver in the vault at Gringotts Wizard Bank. Instead of being penniless, as he thought he was, Harry is suddenly able to buy goodies to share with his new friend Ron, who has no money for such treats.

Kids Wish to Be Empowered by Being Older or Stronger

Harry is dwarfed by his cousin, who is roughly four times his size and a terrible bully. When Harry gets to Hogwarts he discovers that he has untapped magical power. He doesn't get to be older or stronger outright; however, his newly revealed talent for Quidditch garners him the privilege of being selected for the house team during his first year. This honor is comparable to a seventh-grade boy being drafted to play on high school varsity team. People treat Harry as though he is older, which is better than actually becoming older.

Kids Wish to Be Famous

Kids living in a mass-media age long to be known above all. The people they look up to are not local heroes, as in past generations. Chances are good their heroes are internationally known stars of some kind. What kid wouldn't like to imagine waking up one day to find that an entire society somewhere knows his name? Harry, whose guardians make him hide upstairs when they have guests so they won't know he exists, discovers that he is famous! Cool!

Kids Wish to Be Famous in Professional Sports or a Career

Harry is famous for something that happened when he was a baby. But once at Hogwarts, he makes a name for himself by excelling at Quidditch. Other kids in the series are world-famous, such as Viktor Krum, who plays Quidditch for Bulgaria and is just a little older than Harry. Posters and action figures of Viktor abound—but in Harry Potter's magical world, the tiny action figures move around like real people, and the pictures move in live action! Imagine that!

By reading the Harry Potter books, children are allowed to engage in fantasy that also lets their wishes and aspirations take flight. This kindles hope in a child's heart that their wishes—no matter how extravagant—just *might* come true too!

HARRY POTTER APPEALS TO KIDS' LONGING FOR CONTROL

According to *Creating Ever-Cool,* a child has a significant need for control, defined as the ability "to exercise restraint or direction over. Simply put, kids have very little control over the world in which they live. Therefore, they love to gain any measure of control over their sphere of existence. Control touches a strong need that children have to be independent, to make their own choices, to make their own decisions. When they obtain it, kids call it fun."[4]

This need "grows with age, fed each day by every situation that the child cannot control.... When a child realizes he cannot control the things around him, his only recourse is to fantasize that he can."[5]

The Harry Potter books chronicle those years when kids venture out to make their own decisions and choices, moving from dependence on parents to independence and interdependence with peers. As kids identify with Harry and his friends, they can observe Harry, Ron, and Hermione making decisions—some good and some bad—and bearing the consequences.

Albus Dumbledore is a wise mentor who lets Harry face out-of-control situations so that the young wizard can discover the strength, courage, and help he needs to make his way through them. Dumbledore gives Harry advice and direction, empowering Harry to handle situations outside himself. He is there to offer guidance when Harry looks into a magic mirror and sees the deepest desires of his heart. In this way, the readers can reflect on what they would see if they looked into such a mirror: *What is the deepest unfulfilled desire of my heart?* They, too, benefit from Dumbledore's advice: "This mirror will give us neither knowledge or truth. Men have wasted away before it, entranced by what they have seen, or been driven mad, not knowing if what it shows is real or even possible.... It does not do to dwell on dreams and forget to live, remember that."[6]

When it comes to a young person's need for empowerment, Rowling's series offer four attractive elements: magic, secrets, icons, and knowledge.

Magic Is Empowering

Rowling creates situations the characters cannot control, but she places those situations in a fantasy world where Harry and his friends have power and are learning how to use it. Even imaginary magic is empowering! It lets children consider what they would do if they had power in their hands. What kid wouldn't like to imagine having the power to disarm a bully who's about to attack? The kids at Hogwarts realize that the power they have (much like technology in our world) can be used for good or evil. Part of their emerging maturity involves choosing *how* to use the power they are given.

These books are full of fantastic devices that give people power to solve common problems. For instance, a Sneakoscope sounds an alarm to let you know if someone nearby is not trustworthy, a Remembrall is a small ball that glows red if you've forgotten something, and a time-turner allows privileged users to turn back time. Who doesn't enjoy the idea of having a device to solve such pressing problems as knowing who you can trust and feeling like there are not enough hours in the day? Harry also has an Invisibility Cloak that belonged to his father. What kid wouldn't love to imagine donning a cloak of invisibility to explore the world unseen?

Secrets Are Empowering

According to *Creating Ever-Cool,* "If I know a secret, I not only feel special, but I have an invisible control over others who do not know the secret. 'I have a secret and I can't tell you,' is the most powerful phrase on the play-ground. It ensures that those who utter such a sentence will be surrounded and followed until the secret is revealed—instant popularity."[7] Harry discovers power to protect himself from abuse by keeping some information to himself. Since the Dursleys don't know he isn't allowed to use magic away from Hogwarts, they are afraid of what Harry might do at home, so they treat him better than they otherwise would. Ah! There we see the power of a secret!

Every Harry Potter book is full of secrets for Harry, Ron, and Hermione to discover, such as what's in the Chamber of Secrets and what's being hidden at Hogwarts. (I would tell you, but it's a secret. See the power!) At other times, sharing a secret creates a bond of friendship, such as when Harry shares a secret that will help his opponent in an upcoming competition, because he believes that is the fair thing to do. Marketers use the word *secret* when there are hidden features waiting to be revealed, and kids *love it!* Part of the fun of these books is that each one is full of secrets that you know will be revealed by the end. Part of the fun is seeing whether you can discover some of the secrets before Rowling tells you what they are.

Icons Can Be Empowering

Boys especially, but girls also, respond to icons of power. The Nike swoosh is worth millions because it has become an icon associated with athletic power. The lightning bolt scar on Harry's forehead becomes an icon of his power to defeat the evil curse of the villain Voldemort. The Gryffindor symbol of the lion is another icon of power (it can be associated with bravery, the king of beasts, and with Christ himself as the Lion of the tribe of Judah).

Knowledge Is Empowering

Education brings knowledge, and knowledge gives power. Great emphasis is placed on education at Hogwarts, not just to pass tests but to live life well and overcome the forces of evil. Along these lines, kids also love books and maps. Books are the pathway into new knowledge. Maps supply not only knowledge, but also prove useful to gain mastery over the world they must navigate.

Books are revered in the Harry Potter stories. The bookstore where Hogwarts students buy their books is called Flourish and Blotts. It is exquisite, any book-lover's delight! Harry notes, "Even Dudley, who never read anything, would have been wild to get his hands on some of these."[8] Books are the source of important information, without which the good characters could not succeed in their quests.

The books are also a source of imaginative fun. One book that is required for Care of Magical Creatures class is called *The Monster Book of Monsters*. It must be kept in a cage at Flourish and Blotts because it snaps and bites—not only at people but at the other books. You have to stroke its spine to get it to lay open in your hands. Then there is the *Invisible Book of Invisibility*, which the bookstore clerk complains they've never been able to find since their shipment arrived!

According to Del Vecchio, "Maps are special pieces of paper that describe the immense, physical world. They reveal knowledge, which makes a child treat them with awe. And if such a map leads to a buried treasure, then they are coveted; the child who possesses such a document feels powerful."[9] Harry has a special map of Hogwarts that shows several secret passages. It's called a Marauder's Map and is full of helpful features. This map takes on greater significance once Harry realizes who created it—and the implication that he is guided as he ventures out into life by those who went before him, leaving him a helpful map and a heritage of love.

HARRY POTTER APPEALS TO KIDS' DESIRE TO BE THE BEST THEY CAN BE

The book *The Optimistic Child* points out the failure of the self-esteem movement of recent years: "There is no effective technology for teaching feeling good which does not first teach doing well. Feelings of self-esteem in particular, and happiness in general, develop as side effects—of mastering challenges, working successfully, overcoming frustration and boredom, and winning. The feeling of self-esteem is a byproduct of doing well."[10]

The Harry Potter books contribute to kids' need for self-esteem on two levels. First, reading the books is, in itself, quite an accomplishment given the challenging vocabulary, complexity of the plots, and size of the volumes. When kids say, "I've read [however many books]," they are saying that they have accomplished something praiseworthy. For many kids, these books are the most challenging they have ever read, and they are proud of this accomplishment.

Second, the characters within the books develop real abilities to perform effectively, succeed, master skills, and achieve feelings of competence. Adults do not race in to save the day. The kids have to apply their skills, knowledge, perseverance, bravery, cooperation, reasoning, and whatever strength they have to fight against evil. The kids in the books, like those reading them, have a deep desire to be the best they can be. Each story gives the characters and readers who identify with them a tremendous sense of competence. One character, Neville Longbottom, is not competent at much of anything, and yet Rowling finds a way in *The Sorcerer's Stone* to honor his efforts to do what is right, thus allowing him to contribute significantly to the success of his house.

All four stories stress the concept of getting better with practice and achieving a noble goal by hard work. We see that Harry has a gift for playing Quidditch, but we also see him get up at the crack of dawn and spend long hours after school practicing with his team. We see them practice in terrible weather, regardless of the discomfort. We see them persist in the face of foul play by the Slytherin team and veiled attempts to knock Harry off his broom. All of this is part of their determined efforts to win the House Cup, the highest annual Hogwarts honor.

Moral lessons are a crucial part of this sense of accomplishment. Kids are in the process of trying to codify lessons and learn the rules of life that will help them succeed. The Harry Potter books offer many lessons kids can pick up as they read. Some of these lessons are overt, as when Professor Dumbledore instructs Harry directly, but many of them are learned through the assumptions kids make and must discard as the truth is revealed.

HARRY POTTER APPEALS TO KIDS' THRILL IN VICTORY

All kids love to compete and win. In Harry Potter there is plenty of competition on every level: academic and athletic, solo and group, physical and moral. Rowling realizes that girls want to compete and win on all fields. Girls have a place in athletics (three of the players on Gryffindor's Quidditch team are girls) and academics (no one comes close to Hermione). Hermione makes a strong intellectual female lead with a subtle beauty that Ron and Harry don't notice until she's asked to the Yule Ball by one of their sports heroes. When that happens, we see the kind of competition for the attention of the opposite sex that is at the heart of life in middle school and high school.

Of course, the competition between good and evil is pervasive in these stories. Kids long for strength and power to vanquish evil foes, real or imaginary. As long as parents are able to distinguish the fantasy witchcraft and wizardry of Hogwarts as being separate and unrelated to occult practices forbidden by the Bible (i.e., there is no such thing as "good witchcraft"; see chapter 7) these stories can be taken as classic tales of good versus evil.

HARRY POTTER APPEALS TO KIDS' DEEPLY FELT EMOTIONS

One of the strongest attractions of these books is how Rowling deals with the characters' emotions. She neither dismisses nor diminishes the intense emotions they feel. Children and youth experience deeply felt emotions: heartaches, shame, intense fears, anger. In real life these are often discounted, overlooked, or censured. Not only that, but these intense emotions often spring from situations over which kids have no control: families disintegrating, betrayal of trust, life's unfairness, poverty, social problems, and other crushing situations kids shouldn't have to deal with, but do! Kids may not dare to show negative feelings: the depth of their rage, feelings of vengeance, even hatred. They may hide such feelings, but that doesn't make the feelings go away.

The Bible teaches us to grow in self-control, but even adults have some growing to do before mastering these kinds of intense emotions. For kids, especially kids who have been taught not to express such overpowering emotions, facing the depth of their true feelings can be terribly scary. Many children also suffer from overwhelming depression, shame, or despair, which leads some to suicide. The inner life of kids today can be dangerous territory, and they know it. But they may not know how to process such intense and terrifying emotions.

The Harry Potter series acknowledges a wide range of these emotions, but the kids find ways to deal with them. Readers watch the characters progressively bring their out-of-control—even unmentionable—emotions under control. Early on, Harry has outbursts of anger toward those who criticize his dead parents. He rages against those he believes are responsible for their deaths. Ron has to be held back when a rival publicly humiliates him over his family's poverty. Hermione dissolves into tears when Ron and Harry make fun of her. The author treats these feelings with the honesty they deserve. She does not berate the characters for feeling the way they do, but she does show the inherent danger of letting emotions drive their actions. She also shows kids, through the choices and growing self-control of the characters, that other kids feel as deeply as they feel.

Rowling deals especially well with two of the most powerful and dangerous emotions that entrap kids: depression/despair, and fear. In both cases she creates creatures that personify these feelings: Dementors embody terrible depression, and a boggart embodies fear. In both cases, she allows the reader to associate his or her own deepest emotional adversary with these fantasy creatures before showing the characters in the stories how to face and defeat each one. She is clear that both are dangerous, but that they can be faced and overcome successfully.

A boggart is a shape-shifter, taking on the form of whatever one fears most. It is fought with a Riddikulus charm, which turns the boggart into a humorous-looking creature that causes laughter. Boggarts can't sustain themselves while being laughed at. Thus, kids are granted an opportunity to identify and face their greatest fears, along with the idea that there might be a way to transform what frightens them into something that makes them laugh. Likewise, with the dementors, Rowling allows the reader to see how Harry and his friends wrestle with deeply disturbing emotions while fighting off their potential danger.

Harry Potter Appeals to Kids' Need to Conquer Fear

Kids need to know they can face and conquer their fears. Eleanor Roosevelt said, "You gain strength, courage, and confidence by every experience in which you really stop to look fear in the face." This is a truth every kid needs to learn, especially in this dangerous world where violence against children is staggering. Kids may live in a "safe" neighborhood, but they watch the news. They've heard of Polly Klaas, and they know that there are real monsters out there in the world—real dangers too terrifying to dwell on. As Christians, we can offer kids a relationship with a powerful and loving God to help them deal with their fears. But kids need help to face these fears and not give in to them so they can live productive lives.

Paradoxically, children seem to enjoy scary stories. Why? Because entertaining the story can help children move through fear to resolution. Some people have tried to protect children from their fears by removing the scary or violent content. Granted, we need to be sensitive not to create fear for children, especially at certain ages, but sometimes censoring a scary scene—say where the monster or villain is killed at the end of a fairy tale—leaves kids with *unresolved* fears. They need the story to have a climactic ending where the monster is destroyed, so that they can rest easier. They know when the story is over that the monster isn't out there somewhere biding its time. Del Vecchio writes:

> Storytelling has traditionally used fears as a central part of both conflict and resolution. *Kidnapped,* a masterpiece written by Robert Louis Stevenson in the late 1800s, is one such tale. It is a wonderful piece of literature whose very core touched a timeless fear buried deep within the child: that of being stolen from your home.... But the hero of this story, and so many others Mr. Stevenson wrote about, faced a fear and resolved it.... And every kid who reads this story

from generation to generation imagines that he, too, if put in a similar position, could beat that danger as well. Stories such as these put the fear in a child's face and show that, through bravery, endurance, skill, and intelligence, the fear can be resolved.[11]

Fears are challenging. Facing those fears and beating them are grand for the child. It makes him feel older and more mature. So stories that help kids process fear serve a useful purpose.

The Harry Potter books are not the only fantasy stories for children that are criticized for frightful or violent aspects. This has been a chief objection to C. S. Lewis's Chronicles of Narnia, which are routinely suggested by Christians as alternatives to the Harry Potter stories. *Companion to Narnia* by Paul F. Ford states:

> Lewis uses battle imagery.... [He] felt that life is violent, and to deny that would be wrong. He was a long-time reader of G. K. Chesterton, who anticipates Lewis's feelings in the essay "The Red Angel":
> "...a lady has written me an earnest letter saying that fairy tales ought not to be taught to children even if they are true. She says it is cruel to tell children fairy tales, because it frightens them.... All this kind of talk is based on that complete forgetting of what a child is like.... Exactly what the fairy tale does is this: it accustoms [the child] for a series of clear pictures to the idea that these limitless terrors have a limit, that these shapeless enemies have enemies, that these strong enemies of man have enemies in the knights of God, that there is something in the universe more mystical than darkness, and stronger than fear."[12]

I believe each parent must know his or her own child, know the content of what the child is reading, and make wise decisions regarding how the child is affected by frightful aspects of such stories. You may be surprised to find that reading stories that have frightful aspects but allow kids to face fear may have an unexpectedly positive effect. While Harry Potter books were being debated on CNN's *Talkback Live*, a Catholic priest called in with this to contribute from his experience:

> I find the books wonderfully valuable to teach young children about the fact that there is evil in the world. Wait until you've held a 4-year-old kid in your arms who's dying from a gunshot fired by someone who never even knew his name. Wait until you've had to stand at the bedside of a 7-year-old girl dying of brain cancer and explain to her siblings that, you know, they're not going to see their sister again, that this is a dark and evil thing. That happens. That's the real world, and all of those things have happened to me.
>
> And I find that kids who've read Harry Potter, they come and they ask questions about the dark side and the evil, and they are encouraged by the fact the good, as in Harry Potter himself, always comes out on top, and it gives them a chance to talk about the darker things of life and perhaps come to terms with them in as painless a way as possible. I don't see that in any way negative.[13]

This man's practical experience in ministry backs up the findings of Dr. Glen Aylward, a child psychologist and professor of psychiatry and pediatrics with the SIU School of Medicine in Springfield, Illinois. He told the *State Journal-Register* "that 'learning to handle a little fright in small stages is a part of growing up.' A small fear, faced and overcome, makes way for the real end benefits of pride and accomplishment."[14] This is another reason kids give for loving the Harry Potter books. They are proud to say that they were not frightened of what some adults consider too scary. In their minds, being able to face and conquer frightful circumstances along with Harry and his friends is a badge of courage.

For Christian parents these parts of the stories open wide the door for discussion of what your kids fear and how their fears manifest in their thoughts and lives. They also offer a prime opportunity to teach our children the Bible promises that will help them deal with their fears, like Joshua 1:9: "Have I not commanded you? Be strong and courageous. Do not be terrified; do not be discouraged, for the LORD your God will be with you wherever you go." We can also direct them to the many Bible stories in which people, even kids, faced their fears and foes with God's help and conquered both.

HARRY POTTER APPEALS TO KIDS' DESIRE TO BELONG

All children desperately need a sense of their own identity, a sense that they are somehow connected to a family, to friends, and even to God—to someone out there somewhere who knows their name, knows they exist, knows their circumstances, and cares about them. It's even better if kids come to believe that there is a place where they belong, and someday they will be led to that place.

Harry Potter's story does this beautifully in a way that ties in something else kids love: Kids love to receive mail. When Harry is about to turn eleven, Hogwarts sends him an invitation to attend school. The first letter is addressed to: Mr. H. Potter, The Cupboard under the Stairs, 4 Privet Drive, Little Whinging, Surrey.[15]

Apparently someone out there somewhere not only knows Harry's name, but also knows precisely where he is staying and the conditions in which he is being kept. Uncle Vernon promptly moves Harry from the cupboard to Dudley's second bedroom. The next letter is addressed to him at "The Smallest Bedroom, 4 Privet Drive." As the Dursleys flee to prevent Harry from receiving letters, which continue to multiply, the address on each changes to reflect Harry's exact location, down to the smallest detail. This beautifully illustrates what children desperately need to know: Someone out there *knows their name* and knows *where they live* and *where they belong.* They not only have an identity; they have a destiny as well. And someone out there is calling them toward the place where they belong.

Belonging to a Family

Kids need the love that is found in loving families. Unfortunately, many—perhaps most—children in our society have been deprived of the family life optimal for supplying that kind of secure love. These children may easily identify with Harry, who never knew his parents. They can also see a model of love in the Weasley family. The Weasleys don't have much money, but they have enough love for their big family and Harry, too.

Parents are central to a child's world. Even though Harry's parents are dead, their love for him is commemorated. His mother's love for him, in fact, is what protected him from death as a baby. His longing for his parents is mirrored in the longing all children have for a loving relationship with their own parents. Harry cannot bring his parents back, and many readers struggle with similar feelings, although it may be divorce or abandonment that has left them longing. Still, kids see that Harry finds a place to belong within a family (with the Weasleys and at Hogwarts). Although Harry's own mother cannot meet his need for her, Mrs. Weasley fills in. Even Hermione has her moments when she acts like a mother hen. Madam Pomfrey, the school nurse, is about as motherly as they come; as she bustles about to shoo away intruders and while she comforts and cares for those who are hurt or sick, including Harry.

Belonging to a Company of Friends

This is perhaps one of the most gratifying aspects of the Harry Potter books. Within Hogwarts, Harry finds the companionship of true friends. They surely have their ups and downs, as kids this age do in real friendships, but they learn to be good friends, to work together for the common good, and to make up after the inevitable fights. The lessons of learning to belong to a *good* group of friends speaks volumes. At the beginning, Draco Malfoy—not a boy most parents would want their child hanging around with—offers to be Harry's friend and warns him against hanging around with what he calls the wrong sort. But Harry chooses a better peer group, and that choice makes all the difference. As we know, "Bad company corrupts good morals." The Harry Potter books show kids seeking a place to belong how important it is to pick the right group.

HARRY POTTER APPEALS TO JUST-PLAIN-FUN KID STUFF

Another reason for the series' success that cannot be overlooked is the talent and humor of the author that sets her writing apart, and her ability to make the stories fun for kids.

Kids Love Pets

Every kid who goes to Hogwarts is allowed a pet toad, owl, or cat. The owls deliver the mail (Owl Post), but the kids also find consolation and affection—and unexpected surprises—from their pets. Some turn out to be far more than their owners suspect!

Kids Love Wordplay that Makes Reading Fun

A bowl in Professor Dumbledore's office is called a Pensieve. Swirling within it are Dumbledore's excess thoughts! Considering the meaning of the words pensive and sieve, this is a delightful bit of wordplay. Dumbledore lets his excess thoughts swirl there until he needs them. Likewise, the spells in the Harry Potter books are made up of clever words (*none* taken from real spells). Many of them use Latin terms that reveal their meaning. A Fidelius Charm can help a person keep a secret, and *Expelliarmus!* is a charm that disarms an opponent. All the Harry Potter stories are rich with puns like these.

Kids Love Anything Gross, Coarse, Bizarre, or Disgusting

For some unexplained reason, eight to twelve-year-olds (especially boys it seems) love to laugh at things that are gross. Rowling is skilled at making gross things delight her readers. In one Herbology class, the students have to squeeze Bubo-Tuber Pus out of a magical plant. The thick yellow-green pus is useful in the treatment of acne. She also takes things that are frightfully gross and makes them funny, effectively disarming the fright.

Kids Love Treats

Rowling's magical world is full of treats to tantalize the senses. The feasts are delightful, with food appearing on golden plates and goblets filling themselves. Hogwarts features a magical assortment of candies unknown in our world, including Bertie Bott's Every Flavor Beans—and she does mean *every* flavor, some delightful, some disgusting. And whenever someone goes through a harrowing experience or is hurt, the remedy every child loves is administered: chocolate!

The elements covered in this chapter help explain some of the reasons these stories are so popular with children. As I noted at the beginning of this chapter, I am keenly aware and respectful of the concerns voiced in the Christian community that perhaps there are spiritual forces at work behind the scenes contributing to the phenomenal success of these books. Chapter 1 provided examples of several people who feel strongly that this is the case.

Keeping these concerns in mind, while also considering that the books may qualify as classic literature that effectively appeals to children, one must ask where we as Christians go next. I suggest that we open ourselves to the possibility that the best way to deal with this controversy is not to get mad about Harry, but to accept that sincere Christians can come to different conclusions and still be right before God and at peace with one another. We deal with that in the next chapter.

CHAPTER FIVE

WHAT *WOULD* JESUS DO WITH HARRY POTTER?

Decide for Yourself

What would Jesus do? This question, posed in the Christian classic *In His Steps* by Charles Sheldon, has become so familiar as to be reduced to WWJD? But how do we determine what Jesus *would* do, particularly in the kind of divisive debate where well-versed Christians disagree as they do over Harry Potter? Actually, it is precisely this kind of situation in which the WWJD? question proves most useful. (To take the examination a step further, perhaps you'll consider the more pertinent question *What would Jesus have me do?* as you read on.)

In the fictional story *In His Steps,* a pastor challenges members of his church to take a pledge. For one year they agree to ask *What would Jesus do?* before making any personal decision. They agree to consider what the Bible has to say on the matter, pray about it, ask God for wisdom, seek godly counsel if necessary, then come to their own conclusion on what *they believe* Jesus would do.

The church members necessarily rely on dictates of conscience, because the question put to them is to be a matter of personal reflection before the Lord. They are not to poll their friends to see what *they* think Jesus would do. Nor are they to pry into their friends' business and volunteer their own opinion on another's circumstance. Once an individual gains a conscientious conviction in answer to the personal question *What would Jesus do?* he or she pledges to do it regardless of the consequences.

At one point in the story, a man who owns an establishment that sells hard liquor, wine, and beer asks the question. After prayerful consideration of many passages in the Bible that mention wine, he gains a personal conviction that Jesus would not sell hard liquor used primarily to get people drunk. He decides to discontinue the sale of hard liquor but has no such conviction over selling beer and wine.

At a meeting of the people who took the pledge, he is questioned about his decision by a recovering alcoholic. To the alcoholic, beer and wine represent drunkenness, because whenever he takes even one drink he cannot stop himself until he is drunk. The store owner reminds his friend that he has followed the pledge: He prayerfully considered Scripture and came to a personal and conscientious conviction. In this case, as in many of this nature, the personal history of each individual and what the matter *means* to that person make a difference in each one's answer.

It follows that each person's answer would seem the obvious one—in his or her own mind! Considerable adjustments are required to broaden one's perspective and see that another Christian might not make the same associations and would therefore come to a different decision. It would also take some maturity to see—as is most important for Christian unity—that both decisions, while different in terms of personal boundaries and conduct, could be right before God.

This analogy has significant relevance to the debate about whether Christians should read or allow their children to read or see the Harry Potter stories. You may recall from chapter 3 that whether a person takes a pro or con position depends upon the mental associations that person makes. These positions often reflect the personal experience of the individual. One man even appealed to this as part of his argument, saying, "I know from personal experience that it is not okay." Who can effectively argue with that?

So it is not surprising that Alan Jacobs, a professor of English at a

Christian college, associates Harry Potter primarily with classic literature (see p. 21). For him, the issues are defined by his study of the history of magic and science in literature. Alison Lentini, a writer with the Spiritual Counterfeits Project who has degrees in Romance languages and literatures from Princeton University, also looked at the Harry Potter books from a literary perspective (see p. 24). However, before coming to Christ, she was involved in Wicca and neopaganism. She has personal experience with occult practices that correspond to some of the subjects taught at Hogwarts. For her, the issues are defined by her knowledge of occult practices in our world today. Both referred to and compared the Harry Potter books to the Chronicles of Narnia (although I didn't include those remarks in the excerpts); however, their interpretations of Narnia are also contrary. These two Christian scholars came to entirely different conclusions about Harry Potter. What's more, both wrote convincing arguments to support their cases for and against the books. Furthermore, I believe both of their conclusions are right—*for them!*

It's one thing to see how two people can look at the same work of literature and see two different things. But how can two Christians use the same Bible and come to opposing positions about what is right and still both be right with God? There is a biblical explanation for this covered under the heading of disputable matters (found in Romans 14-15 and 1 Corinthians 8-10, which I will address momentarily). In such cases, where cultural, personal, and spiritual issues overlap, individual Christians must finally agree to disagree. Sincere, Bible-believing Christians, who seek the Lord with all their hearts, can be led by the same Holy Spirit to opposing conclusions. This is not relativism nor situational ethics. This is not compromising our commitment to godly conduct under mere social or political pressure. Instead, this is a personal decision about the appropriateness of disputable conduct. Yes, the Bible does allow for such cases.

As we saw in chapter 1, the issues raised over Harry Potter don't lead to a single "Christian position." Reading Harry Potter is a disputable matter because we are not debating whether it is okay for Christians to practice witchcraft or cast spells. The Christian position on that is clear. We agree that we should never participate in or practice anything listed in Deuteronomy 18:9-14 (see chapter 7). But reading Harry Potter is not the same as practicing witchcraft or even—as some assert—promoting it. However, some can *take it to mean just that.* Therein lies the disputable part of these issues that Christians debate in earnest.

Asking *What would Jesus do with Harry Potter?* can be helpful. But it is only useful in dictating personal choice about personal conduct. It loses its usefulness when we turn it into a rhetorical question to tell someone else what Jesus would have *them* do. The letter to *Christianity Today* from the twelve-year-old boy that I referred to in chapter 1 (see p. 29) revealed that he had seriously considered the issues in light of God's Word and came to a definite conclusion that it would be wrong for him to read Harry Potter. He clearly associated reading the books with involving himself in witchcraft, which the Bible forbids. Therefore, it would be sinful for him to do so.

He took his argument a step further, however, when he wrote: "I can't picture Jesus recommending the Harry Potter series as good reading.... It's so obvious that these books are bad."

Another letter I read also appealed to the WWJD? question, arguing along these lines: "Do you think Jesus would be proud of a parent who gave his or her child such a book?"

Both are posited as rhetorical questions, because to the fully convinced mind, it is not feasible for any true Christian to answer, "Yes! I definitely could see Jesus recommending the Harry Potter books," or to suggest, as *Christianity Today* did, that the books would make great Christmas gifts for Christian kids. As confounding as this may be, it is a fact that when Christians ask themselves *What would Jesus do with Harry Potter?* they come to conclusions as different as the ones found in *In His Steps.*

Asking *What would Jesus do with Harry Potter?* as an open-ended question might elicit some surprising positive responses. Consider these:

- Jesus might read the Harry Potter stories and use them as starting points for parables. He might use kids' interest in the battle between good and evil to explain the ultimate battle between good and evil.
- Jesus might ask kids what they would see if they looked into the Mirror of Erised and listen attentively as they struggled to put into words the deepest desires of their hearts.
- Jesus might look at the multitudes who love the Harry Potter stories in the same way he looked at the multitude who came to him hungry for food. He might tell his disciples to feed them, giving them what they were hungry for on the surface of things (a great story with supernatural aspects) then offer them what they are truly hungry for—him.
- Jesus might look on the multitudes reading Harry Potter as being like sheep without a shepherd, easily led astray. He might take note of their tendency to wander into pastures that don't satisfy the deepest hunger of the human soul and warn them of the dangers of venturing off into witchcraft and wizardry in our world just because it might look fun in Harry's world.
- Just as Jesus noticed and met others' physical needs, he might attend to the earthly needs revealed in the lives of those who identify with the characters in Harry Potter. He might get them talking about Harry Potter and listen to what they identify with most: neglect, poverty, discrimination, abuse, fears, dreams, the pressures to fit in, desires to accomplish something in life, or the stresses of school. Then he might show them how to deal with such real parts of their lives.
- He might talk about how Harry deeply needed love and encouragement, because the people he was left to depend on failed him. He might listen as kids told him about the times when people they depended on failed them, then offer them the love and encouragement they deeply need.

- He might compare the trustworthy goodness of Albus Dumbledore to the infinitely superior goodness of God the Father, stressing that we can find the same kind of reassurance in God, and godly mentors, that Harry finds in his headmaster.

- He might talk about how Hogwarts was a reality in Harry's world the whole time, even though Harry didn't know about it until he accepted the invitation to attend. Then he might tell kids about how his Father's kingdom is a parallel realm within reach in this world. He might talk about how people walk by the door that leads to the "magical realm" of Hogwarts without ever noticing it for what it is, and compare that to how people pass by the entrance to God's kingdom (Jesus, who is the door) without knowing what they are missing. He might even show kids that he is the Way (the "magical" transport) to God's kingdom. He might explain that they can only get into God's kingdom by walking in faith, with absolute confidence in that which is unseen, just like Harry and his friends have to walk through the barrier between platforms nine and ten without getting scared or hesitating. Oh, there's a lot Jesus might do with Harry Potter!

- Jesus, who went to parties with tax collectors and sinners and took flak for it from the religious establishment, might be likely to read a controversial book.

- Jesus might show love and acceptance to the kids who love Harry Potter, never looking down on those who read the books nor casting a sideways glance of disapproval at a kid who wears a Harry Potter T-shirt.

In both cases (positive and negative), WWJD? fails to work as a salvo launched against other Christians who hold a different opinion on a matter of conscience. It only works when individuals who are following Jesus use it to become fully convinced in their own minds.

Moral life in Old Testament times was governed by one rule of guidance: Follow the Law of Moses. The Law regulated every detail of community and personal life: family, diet, personal hygiene, worship, and religious ritual. Since no one could keep the law, much of their religious ritual had to do with blood sacrifices to pay for the times they fell short of keeping the law perfectly.

New Testament believers have a New Covenant, under which the blood of Jesus replaces the need for animal sacrifices. "Come, follow me," Jesus calls throughout the Gospels. After Jesus rose from the dead, he took Peter aside to reveal what life held in store for him. He told Peter that his life would end in martyrdom and glory to God. Then Jesus said to him, "Follow me!" Peter saw John following them and asked, "Lord, what about him?" Jesus answered, "If I want him to remain alive until I return, what is that to you? You must follow me" (see John 21). So, our lives are no longer primarily governed by trying to follow the Law, but in seeking to follow Jesus.

How do we follow Jesus today? After all, he has ascended back to the Father. Jesus didn't leave us alone; he gave us the Holy Spirit, who leads us through daily life. Jesus promised, "But the Counselor, the Holy Spirit, whom the Father will send in my name, will teach you all things and will remind you of everything I have said to you" (John 14:26). Later he said, "But when he, the Spirit of truth, comes, he will guide you into all truth. He will not speak on his own; he will speak only what he hears, and he will tell you what is yet to come" (John 16:13). Therefore, when dealing with disputable matters, we follow the leading of the Holy Spirit, aligning ourselves with the Word of God and our own conscience.

This does not mean that we ever disregard or disobey God's direct commands, such as the clear dictates that we are not to practice witchcraft, divination, sorcery, and the like (which are referred to in the Harry Potter books). It does mean that in subjective matters, including whether it's okay to read a story with such references, we must employ personal discernment. As much as people on all sides of this debate banter about verses of

Scripture, there is no specific passage that says reading about these things in a fantasy story is wrong. It remains a matter of personal discretion.

WHAT SCRIPTURE SAYS ABOUT DEALING WITH DISPUTABLE MATTERS

The Scripture passages we should study in order to effectively deal with the Harry Potter debate haven't been given much attention lately. These are found in Romans 14-15 and 1 Corinthians 8-10. These passages apply to the kind of culturally relevant and spiritually potent debate in which Christians take opposing positions about personal conduct. Every Christian who has to deal with the Harry Potter controversy would benefit from an in-depth study of these passages.

For our purposes, I will lay out the principles that can guide us as we make decisions about Harry Potter. The text to the left is my paraphrase of Paul's words. The notations at the right can help you locate the original in your own Bible:

Some Christians' faith allows them more freedom than others. *Some have a conscientious objection on disputable matters. Paul describes those with stricter limitations as having "weaker faith," but he does not use this term in a derogatory way.*	Rom. 14:1
The one with greater freedom (in this case, the one who feels comfortable reading Harry Potter) must not look down on those whose conscience restricts them.	Rom. 14:3
The one who does not (in our case, read Harry Potter) must not condemn those who do.	Rom. 14:3
Each person should be fully convinced in his own mind.	Rom. 14:5
We must stop passing judgment on fellow Christians. *Judging implies that they are deficient in Christ. We will all stand before the Lord to be judged and be held accountable before God for our conduct. Notice that this directive is not put to one side or the other as are some in this passage. Paul is saying, "Both sides, stop it!"*	Rom. 14:1,4,13

Do not cause a fellow Christian to stumble by leading or provoking him to do something contrary to his conscience.	Rom. 14:13
The same behavior can be right for one Christian and wrong for another.	Rom. 14:14
Those who have freedom in disputable matters should be sensitive not to distress conscientious objectors.	Rom. 14:15-16
The kingdom of God is not a matter of what we conclude on disputable matters. *Instead, it is about righteousness (each of us being right with God in Christ's righteousness and in keeping our consciences clean by right conduct as led by the Holy Spirit), peace (with God and others in the body of Christ), and joy in the Holy Spirit. The context of this verse makes it clear that they were dealing with disputable matters that some Christians considered right and others considered wrong. Therefore, the joy of the Holy Spirit is the joy of a clean conscience and also the joy of Christian fellowship—which was lost when Christians were caught up in judging and condemning each other openly.*	Rom. 14:17
Make every effort to do what leads to peace and the spiritual building up of individual Christians and of the church.	Rom. 14:19
Keep your opinions on disputable matters between yourself and God. *If you have freedom, don't flaunt it before those who are troubled by what you do.*	Rom. 14:20-22
Blessed (happy) is the man who does not condemn himself for what he approves. *Once fully convinced, enjoy your decision! This is in keeping with the "whatever you do" verses in 1 Cor. 10:31 and Col. 3:17, 23. If you can read Harry Potter heartily as unto the Lord and to the glory of God, with all your heart, and commit it to the Lord as in Prov. 16:3, then be happy about it.*	Rom. 14:22
If you have doubts (about Harry Potter), don't (read it). *When in doubt, don't! If doubts remain, you would be in sin to do whatever you doubt, because everything that does not come from faith is sin. This is how something that is not a sin for one person could be a sin for another.*	Rom. 14:23
Aim to build each other up in the body of Christ. *Do this even if you come to different conclusions about the suitability of Harry Potter!*	Rom. 15:2
Accept one another, then, just as Christ accepted you, in order to bring praise to God.	Rom. 15:7

WHEN DID YOU LAST HAVE A ROUSING DEBATE OVER EATING MEAT SACRIFICED TO IDOLS?

Contemporary Christians in Western culture haven't had to struggle much over whether it's sinful to eat meat sacrificed to idols, but the first-century church did. That controversy, which is taken up in 1 Corinthians 8–10, also contains principles that apply directly to today's Harry Potter debate.

The Christian faith was birthed out of Judaism, with a long history of Jewish culture preceding it. The Jews remained separate from the Gentiles (non-Jewish peoples) as a crucial part of their devotion to God. Much of their concept of holiness had to do with not being contaminated by non-Jewish cultures and customs. Among other things, they were not to intermarry with Gentiles, eat certain forbidden foods, or worship idols.

These laws were established with the giving of the Law to Moses on Mount Sinai. The first command God spoke to Moses and wrote on the holy tablets was "You shall have no other gods before me. You shall not make for yourself an idol in the form of anything in heaven above or on the earth beneath or in the waters below. You shall not bow down to them or worship them; for I, the LORD your God, am a jealous God, punishing the children for the sin of the fathers to the third and fourth generation of those who hate me, but showing love to a thousand generations of those who love me and keep my commandments" (Exodus 20:3-6). Historically, idol worship became a snare for the Jewish people (even before Moses returned from Mount Sinai with the Law). Gentile culture, of course, was full of idol worship.

After Jesus ascended to the Father, God revealed a great mystery: Salvation is not only for the Jews, but for all who put their faith in Jesus Christ! This was truly good news to the Gentiles. The apostle Paul, who was raised as a strict Jew in a Hellenistic culture, was appointed by God to take the good news of salvation to the Gentiles (see 1 Timothy 2:7). Preaching the gospel to Gentiles took an entirely different approach from that used to convince Jews, who were trained in the Law of Moses and sought the fulfillment of Old Testament messianic prophecies. You can see this nod to Jewish thinking in the gospel of Matthew, which quotes the Old Testament more than sixty times and stresses the phrase *just as it was written* to prove that Jesus was the fulfillment of these prophecies.

But Gentiles were raised in a culture immersed in idolatry, pagan rituals, and worship of many gods. When Paul preached to Gentiles, he accommodated elements of their culture in several ways, such as by using understandable metaphors and eating their foods that were not sanctioned under Jewish dietary laws. Paul converted many Gentile populations in metropolitan cities far from the influence of Jewish customs. There, new converts raised challenging cultural questions about how to live faithfully in the midst of a pagan culture.

Christian converts in Corinth found themselves facing a controversy that caused division, arguments, and confusion among the body of Christ in that city. Corinth was full of idolatry. Those who became Christians in Corinth turned their devotion away from idols to Jesus Christ. However, they had to apply their new faith in a city where idol worship still permeated every facet of daily life. "Temples for the worship of Apollo, Asclepius, Demeter, Aphrodite and other pagan gods and goddesses were seen daily by the Corinthians as they engaged in the activities of everyday life. The worship of Aphrodite, with its many sacred prostitutes, was a particularly strong temptation."[1] In addition to such temptation, they also had to deal with the question of whether they could eat meat that had been sacrificed to an idol.

The local temples provided a service of butchering and preparing meat for the city. The people would bring the animals to the temple, where it would be sacrificed to an idol. Some of the meat went to the temple priests, some was burnt up, and some was given to the idol worshiper. This meat that had been sacrificed to an idol might be prepared and eaten in a feasting hall there at the temple, or the idol worshiper could take it home. Some that was apportioned to the idolatrous priests made its way to the local meat market, where it was sold to the public.

So a heated debate arose over whether a Christian could eat this meat. The Corinthian Christians finally wrote to the apostle Paul, asking him to settle the question. He did not respond with a clear-cut yes or no. Instead, he said, in essence, "Well, it depends."

Let's touch on the points Paul raised and their relevance to the Harry Potter debate.

What's the Real Question?

It was not "Is it wrong to practice idolatry?" The real question was whether Christians were free to do something closely associated with idolatry.

Neither side of the Harry Potter debate is quibbling over whether Christians should practice witchcraft and cast spells, charms, and so on. The Bible is clear that doing these things in our world is wrong. We are not asking "Can a Christian practice witchcraft?"; we are asking whether Christians are free to read stories that are closely associated with such practices and treat them positively.

In What Ways Do We Expose Ourselves to Unseen Demonic Forces?

Idolatry was popular in that pagan world, and people who practiced it did not believe there was anything wrong with it. They in no way associated their religious rituals and worship of their gods and goddesses with demons. However, those who believed God's Word knew that God declared the real power behind all idols comes from unseen demons (Deuteronomy 32:16-17; Psalm 106:36-37). Paul said, "The sacrifices of pagans are offered to demons, not to God, and I do not want you to be participants with demons"(1 Corinthians 10:20). So they wondered if eating meat sacrificed to an idol made them vulnerable to demonic forces.

Those who are not guided by Scripture may look at all the "magic" in the Harry Potter books and say, "It's just fantasy. None of this is real." They don't even believe that there are real demonic forces at work in our world, much less in Harry Potter's. However, those of us who believe the Bible know that, mixed in with all the imaginative words, mythology, fables, legend, folklore, and fairy tale imagery are some terms that correspond to real occult witchcraft practiced in our world today and clearly forbidden by God.

Knowing that J. K. Rowling says she does not believe in magic troubles many Christians who realize that her disbelief in the power of real witchcraft does nothing to halt the demonic forces that God says are real. Ephesians 6:12 says, "For our struggle is not against flesh and blood, but against the rulers, against the authorities, against the powers of this dark world and against the spiritual forces of evil in the heavenly realms." So we may wonder whether reading the Harry Potter books could open someone up to the demonic forces at work behind the scenes, even—and perhaps especially—if that person does not believe such forces exist.

How Might This Look to Others?

Christians in Corinth had been baptized, publicly announcing their new allegiance to Christ and their denunciation of idol worship. Those who opposed eating meat sacrificed to idols thought that people who saw a Christian eating it might think he condoned or promoted idolatry. Non-Christians might be led astray, thinking that one could be a Christian and still be involved in idol worship.

Today, Christians have asked whether reading the Harry Potter books gives the impression that we allow, condone, promote, or are unconcerned about real occult witchcraft. Some worry that kids who read or view Harry Potter might be misled into thinking that real witchcraft is okay, because plenty of other Christians are "into it." Evidence says this concern warrants careful consideration. In the wake of Harry Potter's popularity, marketers of books and other products are eagerly following the Harry Potter crowd with offerings like "Teen Witchcraft Kits," "A Spell-a-Day Tear-off Calendar" that features real spells, and other products that cross the line into genuine occult involvement.

What Does It Mean to Be Free in Christ?

First-century Christians were just learning about this theological principle. Some asserted their freedom by stating that the idol was nothing to them because there is only one true God, so eating meat sacrificed to idols wasn't an issue. They had no pangs of conscience about it. Others were not sure. Some were so used to thinking in terms of idols in competition with God that their consciences were troubled by the thought of eating sacrificed meat. They directly associated the eating of that meat with the practice of idolatry; one was an extension of the other. For them, to eat meat sacrificed to idols was tantamount to worshiping that idol.

Some Christians say the magic in Harry Potter is not occult because it makes no contact with spiritual forces of darkness in our world.[2] They see it as the same kind of literary magic they have allowed their kids to see in *The Sword in the Stone* or *Sleeping Beauty*, so they feel complete freedom to read the books and don't feel any pang of conscience.

Others—especially those who have had experience with occult practices—are not sure or may be adamantly sure that there is a direct association between the literary magic of Hogwarts and the practice of real witchcraft, so to them one is an extension of the other. Their consciences are troubled by all that is associated with Harry Potter. For Christians with these persuasions, to be involved in any way is tantamount to dabbling in real witchcraft or condoning it.

In his first letter to the Corinthians, Paul settled their dispute with principles they could apply conscientiously (again, look to your Bible for the unparaphrased version):

Don't be a know-it-all.	1 Cor. 8:1
An idol is nothing to the person who serves the one true God.	1 Cor. 8:4-6
Sin within disputable matters depends on how someone thinks of it. *Those who associate eating that meat with worshiping an idol violate their conscience. It's not the act of eating, but what that means to the person that matters.*	1 Cor. 8:7-8
Our freedom in Christ is limited by our sensitivity to other Christians. *Those who have no pangs of conscience must be aware that others who do might see them eating meat sacrificed to an idol—or reading Harry Potter—and be emboldened to do likewise in violation of their conscience. The Christian who exercises freedom in Christ does not sin by eating/ reading, but does sin if that freedom causes a fellow believer to do something he or she believes to be wrong.*	1 Cor. 8:9-13
Out of love for others, we may waive many of our freedoms and rights. *Love for others and sensitivity to the ways in which exercising our rights might cause others to stumble should guide our behavior.*	1 Cor. 9:1-18
We should accommodate ourselves to the cultural sensitivities of those with whom we have relationships, being careful that exercising our freedoms does not cause them to do anything they believe to be wrong within their cultural context.	1 Cor. 9:19-22
Do not participate in idolatry or related sexual immorality. *Here Paul showed his cultural sensitivity by not just pointing the finger at pagan idolatry in a pagan culture, but by reminding them of how the Jews committed idolatry with the golden calf.*	1 Cor. 10:6-10
In fact, *flee* idolatry.	1 Cor. 10:14
Don't eat at McIdol's. *Those who eat at the Lord's table (take communion) commune with the Lord; those who ate sacrifices offered on the Lord's altar as part of religious ritual were connected to the Lord. Therefore, those who ate at feasts in the idol's temple and ate meat sacrificed to idols in that context became part of their religious ritual and were sitting down to dinner with demons! "God's people are warned that if they do eat meat sacrificed to idols, they should not eat it with pagans in their temple feasts, for to do so is to become 'participants with demons.'"3*	1 Cor. 10:16-22
"Everything is permissible," but not everything is beneficial or constructive. *Christians should not only ask "Do I have the right to do this?" but also "How will my actions affect others? Will this work out for their good?" Aim not only to be "right," but also to be beneficial to others and constructive in building up the body of Christ.*	1 Cor. 10:23-24

Then, in 1 Corinthians 10:25-33, Paul makes some specific applications:

> Eat anything sold in the meat market without raising questions of conscience, for, "The earth is the Lord's, and everything in it."
>
> If some unbeliever invites you to a meal and you want to go, eat whatever is put before you without raising questions of conscience. But if anyone says to you, "This has been offered in sacrifice," then do not eat it, both for the sake of the man who told you and for conscience' sake—the other man's conscience, I mean, not yours. For why should my freedom be judged by another's conscience? If I take part in the meal with thankfulness, why am I denounced because of something I thank God for?
>
> So whether you eat or drink or *whatever you do,* do it all for the glory of God. Do not cause anyone to stumble, whether Jews, Greeks or the church of God—even as I try to please everybody in every way. For I am not seeking my own good but the good of many, so that they may be saved" (emphasis added).

So we must make personal decisions in disputable matters on the basis of (1) any commands of Scripture that have legitimate bearing on the issue, (2) applying the scriptural principles and precepts that relate to our freedom in Christ and love for others, (3) the leading of the Holy Spirit, (4) keeping a clean conscience, and (5) operating under the guidance of appropriate God-given authorities in our lives.

Both sides arguing about whether to eat meat sacrificed to idols could cite Scripture and experience to back up their positions. Both sides were sure they were right (on the basis of their convictions), and—judging from the emphasis Paul put on this point in his reply—both sides resorted to judging those of a different opinion as deficient Christians. There was no way for the entire community of faith to come to a conclusion one way or the other. Therefore, God provided guidelines for how we are to treat each other with love and respect while we agree to disagree.

Could the Harry Potter books really be right for one Christian and absolutely wrong for another? Yes! Just as one Christian may be allowed to take a drink of wine or even sell it as part of his business, another Christian may be convicted by the Holy Spirit never to take a sip. Christians who associate the Harry Potter stories with the real occult understandably have doubts about reading them; therefore it would be sinful to do so, according to Romans 14:23. But those who make no such association and who approve of the Harry Potter books without any pang of conscience, can happily do so according to Romans 14:22 without being in sin. We see here scriptural grounds for both positions.

So if you are not convicted about reading the Harry Potter books, go ahead and enjoy them. If you are convicted, do not read them. But neither position can dictate the conscience of another in such disputable matters (see chapter 6 and Galatians 5:13-15 for a discussion about the dangers of judging one another). Furthermore, if you have freedom to read them, learn how you could go on to make it not only lawful for you, but also profitable for the kingdom of God and the spiritual training of children. I'll discuss some of these methods in the coming chapters.

The only position that cannot be upheld by God's Word is to judge, look down upon, or condemn another Christian for coming to a conviction that differs from yours. God tells us all, "Accept one another, then, just as Christ accepted you, in order to bring praise to God" (Romans 15:7). To that I say a hearty, "Amen!" and pray that Christians on both sides of this debate can join me.

Chapter Six

BEWARE THE DANGERS OF THE DEBATE

Subtle Snares that All Christians Need to Avoid

Have you received an e-mail similar to this one? I've abbreviated it somewhat, but this is essentially as I received it. Beware! All the dangers of the debate can be found within it:

> This is the most evil thing I have laid my eyes on in 10 years…and no one seems to understand its threat.
>
> Harry Potter is the creation of a former UK English teacher who *promotes witchcraft and Satanism. Harry is a 13 year old "wizard." [Her] creation openly *blasphemes Jesus and God and promotes sorcery, *seeking revenge upon anyone who upsets them by *giving you examples (even the *sources with authors and titles!) of spells, rituals, and *demonic powers. It is the *doorway for children to enter the Dark Side of evil.
>
> I think the problem is that parents have not reviewed the material. The name seems harmless enough… Harry Potter. But that is where it all ends. Let me give you a few quotes from some of the influenced readers themselves:
>
> "The Harry Potter books are cool, 'cause they teach you all about magic and how you can use it to control people and get revenge on

your enemies," said Hartland, WI, 10-year-old Craig Nowell, a recent convert to the New Satanic Order Of The Black Circle. "I want to learn the Cruciatus Curse, to make my muggle science teacher suffer for giving me a D."

Or how about the REALLY young and innocent impressionable mind of a 6 year old when asked about her favorite character: "Hermione is my favorite, because she's smart and has a kitty," said 6-year-old Jessica Lehman of Easley, SC. "Jesus died because He was weak and stupid."

And here is dear Ashley, a 9 year old, the typical average age reader of Harry Potter: "I used to believe in what they taught us at Sunday School," said Ashley, conjuring up an ancient spell to sum-mon Cerebus, the three-headed hound of hell. "But the Harry Potter books showed me that magic is real, something I can learn and use right now, and that the Bible is nothing but boring lies."

DOES THIS GET YOUR ATTENTION!! If not, how about a quote from a High Priest of Satanism:

"Harry is an absolute godsend to our cause," said High Priest Egan of the First Church Of Satan in Salem, MA. "An organization like ours thrives on new blood—no pun intended—and we've had more applicants than we can handle lately. And, of course, practically all of them are virgins, which is gravy." [Since 1995, open applicants to Satan worship has increased from around 100,000 to now…14 MILLION children and young adults!]

It makes me physically ill, people! But, I think I can offer you an explanation of why this is happening. Children have been bom-barded with action, adventure, thrills and scares to the point Hollywood can produce nothing new to give them the next 'high.' *Parents have neglected to see what their children are reading and doing, and simply seem satisfied that 'Little Johnny is interested in reading.' AND…educators and the NEA are PUSHING this [censored] with NO WARNING as to the effects or the contents.

Still not convinced? I will leave you with something to let you make up your own mind. First the URL to read some background of what I have given you: http://www.onion.com: Harry Potter Books Spark Rise In Satanism Among Children. And finally, a quote from the author herself, J. K. Rowling, describing the objections of Christian reviewers to her writings: WARNING: THE FOLLOWING QUOTE CONTAINS HIGHLY GRAPHIC DESCRIPTIONS OF A PORNOGRAPHIC NATURE AND SHOULD NOT BE VIEWED BY MINORS!

"I think it's absolute rubbish to protest children's books on the grounds that they are luring children to Satan," Rowling told a London Times reporter in a July 17 interview. "People should be praising them for that. These books guide children to an understanding that the weak, idiotic Son Of God is a living hoax who will be humiliated when the rain of fire comes, and will suck the greasy [censored] of the Dark Lord while we, his faithful servants, laugh and cavort in victory."

My hope is that you will see fit to become involved in getting the word out about this garbage. Please FWD to every pastor, teacher, and parent you know. This author has now published FOUR BOOKS in less than 2 years of this *'encyclopedia of Satanism' and is surely going to write more. I also ask all Christians to please pray for this *lost woman's soul. Pray also for the Holy Spirit to work in the young minds of those who are reading this garbage that they may be delivered from its harm. Lastly, pray for all parents to grow closer to their children, and that a bond of sharing thoughts and spiritual intimacy will grow between them. In service to the Lord Jesus, His honor and glory…[1]

The debate over Harry Potter in the Christian community has been contaminated by many errors in our methods of gathering and passing along information, as well as in the truthfulness of what we are believing and acting upon. As a result, our judgments are often skewed and our witness before the world is heavily damaged. Therefore, let's all stop to seriously consider the dangers of this kind of debate. As I address them, see if you can spot them in the preceding e-mail.

BEWARE OF BELIEVING FALSEHOOD AND BUILDING ON IT

Jesus said, "And I will ask the Father, and he will give you another Counselor to be with you forever—the Spirit of truth" (John 14:16-17).

Every quote cited in this e-mail message is entirely fabricated. The message also contains assumptions that are verifiably untrue. Those statements marked with an asterisk (my notations) are not true; in fact, they are unsubstantiated assumptions. Those startling remarks from *fictitious* children were also fictitious. They originated with *The Onion* at Onion.com, which was referenced but apparently not checked closely. *The Onion* is a satirical page that's like a cross between an R-rated *Mad* magazine and tabloid papers. It features outrageous stories about things like alien conventions or obese people winning $135 million lawsuits against Hershey's.

Their disclaimer states: "*The Onion* is a satirical newspaper published by Onion, Inc. *The Onion* uses invented names in all its stories, except in cases when public figures are being satirized. Any other use of real names is accidental and coincidental. The contents of this web-site—graphics, text and other elements—is © Copyright 2000 by Onion, Inc., and may not be reprinted or retransmitted in whole or in part without the expressed written consent of the publisher. *The Onion* is not intended for readers under 18 years of age."

When *The Onion* published its satirical information about Harry Potter,

Onion.com was lampooning fears voiced by the Christian community. Almost anyone who had read the books would easily recognize these statements as ludicrous. However, many passing it on took them as further reason *not* to read the books. Consequently, they had no reference against which to gauge its truthfulness. Anyone who checked the source would have seen that Onion.com's article was a hoax, but many did not. Instead, they heeded the call to action by forwarding an untrue and misleading message in cyberspace, unintentionally lending their credibility and good name to something contrary to truth. How the world and the devil must laugh at us when we are duped into believing and spreading lies in the name of Jesus.

Many people sent e-mail to Rowling's publisher, Scholastic, with concerns over the slanderous quotes attributed to Rowling. Here is Scholastic's reply:

> Thank you for your e-mail. We are pleased to respond.
>
> This quote was contained in an article in *The Onion. The Onion* is a satirical publication and this article is a completely fictional piece. The quotes in the article are also fictional, including the false and offensive statements attributed to J. K. Rowling. Obviously, the article does not reflect the views of Scholastic or J. K. Rowling.
>
> We thank you for bringing this matter to our attention. Scholastic takes seriously its mission to encourage children to read and is thrilled that millions of children, their parents and teachers are reading the Harry Potter books.

Moreover, some have built a scriptural response on a shaky foundation of falsehood. The writer of the e-mail quoted Colossians 2:8 (NASB), "See to it that no one takes you captive through…empty deception," even while being deceived. The writer also cited 2 Thessalonians 2:10, "They perish because they refused to love the truth," while apparently not loving the truth enough to check out these scandalous statements. No matter how many Bible verses we use, if we use them to build a foundation of falsehood, the enemy can undermine the work of God. That is dangerous indeed! We have plenty of valid concerns to discuss in this debate without spending our time reacting to false information.

How to Deal with This Danger

Seek truth. Be sure to check questionable e-mails at http://www.Truthor Fiction.com. This Web site is hosted by Rich Buhler, a reputable minister and veteran radio host. TruthorFiction.com checks rumors back to at least two credible sources. They have other valuable articles related to Harry Potter and an excellent article *about* rumors.

Use common sense and check the source. The pornographic quote ascribed to J. K. Rowling was reportedly from *The London Times*. Even if people consider the remark consistent with what a Satanist would say—although Rowling is not a Satanist—common sense would question whether a reputable newspaper would publish such obscenity. A visit to the archives at www.LondonTimes.com for July 17 would have revealed that the quote was false.

Don't rely solely on someone else's summary of these complex issues. For example, *New Man* magazine concluded one of its articles on Harry Potter with these remarks: "Dads with kids aching to meet Harry and who wisely turn to trusted resources may, however, find themselves in a tangled thicket of conflicting opinions. Focus on the Family's Linda Beam says 'It is best to leave Harry Potter on the shelf,' while *World* magazine critic Roy Maynard claims that 'Rowling…keeps it safe, inoffensive, and non-occult.'"[2]

There's a big problem with this summation. To start with, the quote attributed to "Linda Beam" is actually from *Lindy* Beam. In its proper context, her remarks about keeping Harry Potter on the shelf read as follows: "So what are Christian parents to do with Harry Potter? The books could be a springboard to fruitful discussion to prevent children from falling into…errors. But parents should evaluate the books to determine if the series is appropriate for the age and maturity of their own children. If you feel that through reading Harry Potter your children might develop 'an excessive and unhealthy interest' in wizardry and magic, then the answer is simple: Leave the books on the shelf."[3] The author of the *New Man* piece unwittingly proved his point that there is indeed "a tangled thicket of conflicting opinions"—further affirmation that responsible and concerned parents dare not rely solely on someone else's summary. The summary itself could prove inexact and misleading, even while appealing to the credibility of a trusted and reputable organization like Focus on the Family.

Beware of Talking Like the Devil

Titus 3:2 commands us "to slander no one." Leviticus 19:16 says, "Do not go about spreading slander among your people." Even our Lord Jesus included slander as one of the evils about which he said, "All these evils come from inside and make a man 'unclean'" (Mark 7:23). These and many other Bible verses rebuke slander, which is false accusations and hurtful innuendo.

Given the nature of the debate and our aim to protect people from the work of the devil, it is significant that the Greek word translated "slanderer" is *diabolos*. It is taken from the same root as the word for the devil, or *accuser*. So a slanderer is one who speaks like the devil by spreading false accusations. In our efforts to destroy the works of the devil, let's make sure we're not deceived into speaking like him.

A related error occurs when false accusations, personal assumptions, and slanderous remarks incite others to react. Repeating false accusations does not make them true; however, sometimes accusations are repeated so often (such as the accusation that Rowling is a Satanist) that the accuser has established a lie as truth in some minds.

J. K. Rowling has repeatedly and consistently stated that she has no interest in or involvement with Satanism. In October 1999, she told CNN.com *Book News*, "I absolutely did not start writing these books to encourage any child into witchcraft. I'm laughing slightly because to me the idea is absurd." She also said, "It is a fantasy world and they understand that completely."[4]

Katie Couric interviewed J. K. Rowling on NBC's *Today Show* October 20, 2000:

Katie: I'm not sure if we should bite this off, but I'm going to anyway. Tammy in Kansas was wondering what would encourage you to write books for children that are supporting the devil, witchcraft, and anything that has to do with Satan? You've heard that before.

J. K.: Well nothing would encourage me to do that, because I haven't done it so far. So, why would I start doing it now?

Some dismiss Rowling's clear denials, assuming that she is a deceiver. She told Larry King that she thought some of the people making such accusations must not have read the books. This is true. Many who are the most vocal critics of Harry Potter have not read the books because they have mentally filed them as "witchcraft." Since the accusations are really against the books as well as the author, I reread the first three books just to see if any of the stories mention anything about Satanism, the devil, or demonic forces as we know them. Rereading the books confirmed my initial conclusion (and Charles Colson's): There is no contact with Satan or the devil, not even by the evil characters in Harry Potter. You can verify this yourself.

The books to date contain only two references to the devil: an exclamation by Harry's Uncle Vernon—"What the Devil!"—made outside the world of Hogwarts, and a fictitious plant called "Devil's Snare" that entangles characters in its tendrils and can be defeated with light. There are no statements in these books mentioning, supporting, or encouraging contact with Satan, the devil, or demons. This association has been placed upon the books by those who choose to define the fantasy terminology by equating some terms and practices with their occult parallel (see chapter 3). After making that association, they conclude that the books encourage Satanism.

The interview with Katie Couric continued:

Katie: You have heard of criticism along those lines, ever since the beginning. I think it grew as more and more books came out.

J. K.: A very famous writer once said, "A book is like a mirror. If a fool looks in, you can't expect a genius to look out." People tend to find in books what they want to find. And I think my books are very moral. I know they have absolutely nothing to do with what this lady is writing about, so I'm afraid I can't give her much help there.

Are you offended by her implication that people who make such assumptions appear foolish? We earned that comment. I have been monitoring what Christians have been saying about Rowling for a long time. Her remarks are much more reserved and kind toward her accusers than their tone and accusations generally are of her.

How to Deal with This Danger

Look into God's mirror. Another famous writer (God) wrote: "Do not merely listen to the word, and so deceive yourselves. Do what it says. Anyone who listens to the word but does not do what it says is like a man who looks at his face in a mirror and, after looking at himself, goes away and immediately forgets what he looks like. But the man who looks intently into the perfect law that gives freedom, and continues to do this, not forgetting what he has heard, but doing it—he will be blessed in what he does. If anyone considers himself religious and yet does not keep a tight rein on his tongue, he deceives himself and his religion is worthless" (James 1:22-26).

We need to look into God's Word and consider whether we have sinned by slandering, gossiping, spreading false assumptions, or talking like the accuser. Even if we acted on misleading information, we need to ask the Holy Spirit to help us keep a tight rein on our tongues.

"Produce fruit in keeping with repentance" (Matthew 3:8). God's Word is given for reproof and correction. If we've passed on accusations, assumptions, or slanderous remarks, we should try to undo the damage. Most appropriately, we must tell anyone to whom we've passed such messages that we were misinformed. Then we need to commit ourselves to verifying the truth in fact before we speak.

Beware of Giving In to the Sinful Nature

God condemns sorcery and witchcraft as "acts of the sinful nature" in Galatians 5:19-20 (NIV). What God condemns, we ought also to condemn. In our sincere zeal to oppose witchcraft, however, we may have fallen into several other traps the Lord lists in the same passage as acts of our sinful nature: "When you follow the desires of your sinful nature, your lives will produce these evil results:… participation in demonic activities, hostility, quarreling…outbursts of anger…divisions, the feeling that everyone is wrong except those in your own little group…. Let me tell you again, as I have before, that anyone living that sort of life will not inherit the Kingdom of God. But when the Holy Spirit controls our lives, he will produce this kind of fruit in us: love, joy, peace, patience, kindness, goodness, faithfulness, gentleness, and self-control. Here there is no conflict with the law" (Galatians 5:19-23, NLT).

This danger involves *the spirit in which* we debate and the effects it produces. When hostility and derision fly back and forth among Christians, respectful debate turns into disgrace. One letter to the editors of *Christianity Today* regarding their editorial "Why We Like Harry Potter" read:

"Do you have Wiccans on your staff? Are you seriously supporting this book? And I thought Benny Hinn was weird."[5]

We all operate from our sinful nature sometimes, but let's remember: God puts enmity, strife, dissension, factions, and disputes in the same category as sorcery. Fighting against one cannot justify the others.

How to Deal with This Danger

Serve one another in love. The way to deal with this danger—and a warning—is found a few verses earlier: "You, my brothers, were called to be free. But do not use your freedom to indulge the sinful nature; rather, serve one another in love. The entire law is summed up in a single command: 'Love your neighbor as yourself.' If you keep on biting and devouring each other, watch out or you will be destroyed by each other" (Galatians 5:13-15). Also, keep in step with, or "walk" in, the Holy Spirit, and you will not give in to the sinful nature. Appeal to the Holy Spirit to help us all!

BEWARE OF JUDGING ONE ANOTHER

Let's not confuse judging each other with exercising sound judgment. The apostles and elders of the early church exercised sound judgment in Acts 15 when deciding an important but disputable church matter (whether Christians should be circumcised). In a similar way, we should use wisdom, godly counsel, and sound judgment when thinking through disputable matters (see chapter 5). Romans 14 doesn't state that we shouldn't think things through. Instead, it warns against the type of judgment that discredits a person rather than examines the issues: "You, then, why do you judge your brother? Or why do you look down on your brother?" (verse 10). This kind of passing judgment was posed by one reader of a Christian magazine that printed favorable statements about Harry Potter: "What part of the Bible don't you understand?"

Here are some unfortunate ways in which we have publicly judged one another (rather than the issues):

THOSE WHO OPPOSE THE SERIES HAVE SAID THAT THOSE WHO ARE FAVORABLE:	THOSE FAVORABLE TOWARD THE SERIES HAVE SAID THAT THOSE WHO OPPOSE IT:
• Have given in to peer pressure or political correctness	• Are too closed-minded to read the books
• Are spiritually lax	• Are ignorant about literature
• Don't believe there's a devil or demonic spirits at work today	• Are fanatical and hysterical
• Care more about fitting in with culture than they care about their children's spiritual well-being	• Make Christians look stupid
• Are not "real" Christians, or at least are "certainly not Spirit-filled"	• Have bought into ridiculous "conspiracy theories"
• Have been deceived by Satan	• Are governed by unnecessary fear
• Don't know God's Word well enough to recognize the dangers of witchcraft	• Are uninformed
	• Act only on hearsay

How to Deal with This Danger

Stop passing judgment! Simply put, we should consider how we feel when we are judged, reflect upon the division it causes, and then apply the Golden Rule. Whenever we hear ourselves saying, "They must be…," *stop*. Let's turn our attention to the issues rather than to discrediting fellow Christians.

Determine not to quarrel over Harry Potter. If someone wants to discuss or share emerging ideas, make sure it doesn't digress into personal attacks.

BEWARE OF THE DANGER OF FOOLISH AND STUPID ARGUMENTS

"Don't have anything to do with foolish and stupid arguments, because you know they produce quarrels. And the Lord's servant must not quarrel; instead, he must be kind to everyone, able to teach, not resentful. Those who oppose him he must gently instruct, in the hope that God will grant them repentance leading them to a knowledge of the truth, and that they will come to their senses and escape from the trap of the devil, who has taken them captive to do his will" (2 Timothy 2:23-26).

No Christian wants to be taken captive to do the devil's will. When reading this passage, our first inclination may be to apply it to our opponents or dismiss it because the issues related to Harry Potter are important. However, the *way* we argue can be foolish and stupid. Therefore, we all need to be kind to everyone, deal with each other gently, in the hopes God will grant us repentance—if necessary—leading to a knowledge of the truth. If we fall into a snare, we need to come to our senses and help each other escape from the trap of the devil, who may have taken us captive to do his will instead of God's.

No one wants to fall into a snare, so let's be alert for these:

"Meteoric Leaps" to illogical conclusions. Some Christians suggest that reading Harry Potter could lead kids to commit atrocious acts like the Columbine massacre. Their reasoning begins with an assumption and goes like this: (1) Harry Potter leads kids into Satanism. (2) Eric Harris and Dylan Klebold (who murdered their classmates at Columbine High School) were into Satanism. (3) Therefore, some who read Harry Potter could be led to kill their classmates.

A guest on CNN's *Talkback Live* asserted such a line of reasoning related to the Harry Potter books. Host Bobbie Battista called it "a meteoric leap" and confronted the faulty logic. The media has been open to hearing from those who object to Rowling's books, but when we squander such an opportunity with meteoric leaps of logic, the world will dismiss us, and we may lose future opportunities to be heard on valid concerns.

Circular reasoning. No one can successfully reason with someone using a circular argument. In the Harry Potter debate it begins with an assumption and goes like this: (1) J. K. Rowling is a Satanist. (2) Satan is a deceiver and disguises himself as an angel of light. (3) Therefore, Rowling is a deceiver. (4) She claims not to support Satanism, and no evidence links her to Satanism. (5) This lack of evidence proves she is deceiving us, because she is a Satanist. (6) Therefore...what? Some would actually say she's a witch!

One Christian who held this view said, "Well, you can't expect her to market pentagrams *outright.*" Such reasoning dismisses all statements that do not support the original assumption as deceptive. When told that Rowling has stated she does not believe in magic and does not want to lead children into witchcraft, the CNN *Talkback Live* guest replied, "Well, that's what she *says.*"

In another case, a woman reacting to a favorable Harry Potter article in a Christian magazine told the managing editor, "You can tell J. K. Rowling is a witch."

"How?" the editor asked.

"She looks like one. Didn't you see her boots?"

What can one say to that? I say it's a good thing J. K. Rowling doesn't have a wart!

C. S. Lewis terms this kind of reasoning error "Bulverism." *C. S. Lewis: A Companion and Guide* offers this definition:

BULVERISM: This idea comes from the essay **"Bulverism": or, the Foundation of 20th Century Thought** in which Lewis says: "You must show *that* a man is wrong before you start explaining *why* he is wrong. The modern method is to assume without discussion *that* he is wrong and then distract his attention from this (the only real issue) by busily explaining how he became so silly...I have found the device so common that I have had to invent a name for it. I call it Bulverism. Some day I am going to write the biography of its imaginary inventor, Ezekiel Bulver, whose destiny was determined at the age of five when he heard his mother say to his father—who had been maintaining that two sides of a triangle were together greater than the third—'Oh you say that *because you are a man.*' 'At that moment,' E. Bulver assures us, 'there flashed across my opening mind the great truth that refutation is no necessary part of argument. Assume that your opponent is wrong, and then explain his error, and the world will be at your feet. Attempt to prove that he is wrong or (worse still) try to find out whether he is wrong or right, and the national dynamism of our age will thrust you to the wall.' That is how Bulver became one of the makers of the Twentieth Century."[6]

Basing arguments and judgments on selective quotes. The examples in the following pages demonstrate that tightly edited passages lifted from their contexts can present frightful misrepresentations of stories and authors' intentions. Allow me to demonstrate by considering a few quotes.

Would you deem these scenes of violence suitable in a children's book?

[The hero] slashed his legs from under him and, with the back-cut of the same stroke, walloped off his head.[7]

A dull, grey voice...replied, "I'm hunger. I'm thirst. Where I bite, I hold till I die, and even after death they must cut out my mouthful from my enemy's body and bury it with me.... I can drink a river of blood and not burst. Show me your enemies."[8]

Harry Potter? No. Narnia. Both quotes are taken from *Prince Caspian.* In the case of Harry Potter, opponents have pulled similar quotes from the books to suggest that they glorify murder. The same could be done with any work—consider what selective excerpts from the account of Saul's death in 1 Samuel 28–31 might miscommunicate. In context, however, the Harry Potter passages in question show the violence of evil and demonstrate the good side bravely standing against those with murderous intent.

How do the following passages hold up as appropriate reading for children?

"Call her up," said the grey voice. "We are all ready. Draw the circle. Prepare the blue fire."…

"So that is your plan…! Black sorcery and the calling up of an accursed spirit."[9]

"I mean the Witch. Sit down again. Don't all take fright at a name as if you were children. We want power: and we want a power that will be on our side."[10]

"[O]ut of the water came a great wet, bearded head, larger than a man's, crowned with rushes.… [O]ut of its mouth a deep voice came."

"Hail, Lord," it said. "Loose my chains."

"Who on earth is *that*?"…

"I think it's the river-god, but hush,"…

"Bacchus,"… "Deliver him from his chains."[11]

Again, these passages are taken from the Narnia series. Many object to Harry Potter because the stories use terminology ascribed to Wicca or used in occult practices. Their arguments are based on the idea that a term can be removed from its fantasy setting and assigned the same meaning held by the term in the real world, assuming that the real-world definition is an author's *intended* meaning (see chapter 3). People who make such associations certainly have some basis to do so, since the Harry Potter books are replete with terms used in occult practices. People who do this, however, should draw similar parallels for all fantasy, even that written by Christians. In the passages above, Lewis uses several occult terms. Wicca involves nature worship and calling up gods and goddesses of the earth and rivers. Bacchus, you may remember, is the mythological figure associated with debauchery and drunkenness. Must we say, then, that Lewis's stories promote Wicca and conclude that they are unsuitable for children and Christians? If we take this position about the Harry Potter stories, then the answer is yes.

This error is partly responsible for generating concerns that Harry Potter leads children into witchcraft. There are passages in both series that have potential to cause confusion and that lend themselves to clarification. By the same token, both series could also be perused for quotes that would create a favorable impression of the books. That is why it is best—especially when reviewing fantasy literature—to actually read one of the stories and see all quotes in context. Let's take a look at this principle in light of another faulty argument:

Inconsistent application of criteria. Questions often arise as to why some denounce Harry Potter but find the Chronicles of Narnia, *The Hobbit,* and the Lord of the Rings acceptable. The most common answer is that the fantasy of Lewis and Tolkien is good because the authors were Christians writing within a Christian framework. Indeed they do. In fact, the Narnia series is often lauded by Harry Potter opponents as more suitable reading material.

However, if objections to the books concern the following elements, the same complaints should apply to any book, regardless of the author's spiritual orientation: violent content, terminology representative of occult practices (spells, using a crystal ball, references to astrology, etc.), and the use of "good magic" by the heroes (implying that there is such a thing as "good magic" or "good witchcraft"). For purposes of this discussion, I will restrict comparison between the Narnia and Potter series to these elements; there are of course other points of comparison.

If violence, occult terms, and "good" witchcraft are the complaints against Harry Potter, does it make sense to sanctify these same elements in books authored by Christians? All three elements appear in Lewis's and Tolkien's books. If these things are wrong, wouldn't they be doubly wrong if condoned by a Christian? One could argue that a Christian should be more trustworthy and therefore more likely to lead children astray in matters such as these. Doesn't consistency dictate applying our objections to all stories with these elements?

Some may assume that because Lewis and Tolkien were Christians, their faith curbed that which critics of Harry Potter object to today. However, this is not the case. Some opponents extract tightly edited quotes from Rowling's books to prove their point. The same faulty tactics would likewise discredit Narnia and other works of fantasy by Christians.

A third major complaint is that heroes in Harry Potter use "good magic" and may therefore lead kids to think there is such a thing as "good witchcraft." A related concern is that because Harry and his friends use so-called white magic to solve their problems, readers are encouraged to do the same. Many presume that the Narnia stories are exempt from this criticism because only the villains use magic; this is not so. In Narnia, "good magicians" use "good magic," including astrology, crystals, and spells.

In *Voyage of the Dawn Treader*, Lucy (the heroine) must read a book of spells to break the enchantment over the Duffers. She is compelled to do so but does not refuse. In the process, she is lured into learning other spells. Even though Aslan later points out the dangers, she did give in to temptation. Then, after using the "right" spell to make the Duffers visible, she discovers that Coriakin, who is presumed to be an evil magician, is really a good magician working for Aslan (the Christ figure).

In *Prince Caspian*, Doctor Cornelius (one of the heroes) is asked, "How ever did you find us out?" He replies, "By a little use of simple magic, your Majesty.... I had a pretty good guess from my crystal as to where I should find you."[12]

In *Companion to Narnia*, Paul F. Ford writes:

Magic at first calls to mind various evil enchanters, enchantments, and instruments we encounter in Narnia....

But the wardrobe that lets the children into Narnia is also magic; there is a hint from Lewis that good magic may have chased them into Narnia, and Narnia knows good magicians like Coriakin and Doctor Cornelius.... In short, the *Chronicles* do not present a battle between the ordinary, natural scene and dark, unnatural magical powers. The ordinary, natural scene is rather the battlefield on which the good magic confronts the bad, just as ultimately the human heart is the stage on which the mystery of grace wrestles with the mystery of evil....

Lewis spoke in *"The Weight of Glory"*: "Do you think I am trying to weave a spell? Perhaps I am; but remember your fairy tales. Spells are used for breaking enchantments as well as for inducing them. And you and I have need of the strongest spell that can be found to wake us from the evil enchantment of worldliness which has been laid upon us for nearly a hundred years."[13]

Astrology can also be found in *Prince Caspian:* "He [a Centaur on the good side] was a prophet and star gazer and knew what they had come about."[14] *Companion to Narnia* notes, "As befits a medieval universe, the portents of astrology are taken seriously, and Centaurs are especially good at reading these omens in the heavens."[15] So too, in Harry Potter the references to astrology and Centaurs (who live in the Forbidden Forest) are connected.

I am not arguing that fantasy stories by respected Christian authors should be either thrown out as evil or wholeheartedly embraced. That, too, is a matter of personal conviction. My aim here is to point out that decrying the Harry Potter books for these reasons while making allowances for the very same things in the writings of Lewis (and Tolkien or anyone else) is inconsistent. Can kids really make such a sophisticated distinction between "wrong" elements in Harry Potter and the same elements placed in a "Christian moral context"? Even if kids did comprehend that astrology and such in Narnia was done under Aslan's authority, it could be argued that, logically, such practices might be permissible if exercised under Jesus' authority in our world. We know from the Bible, however, that this is not true. It is *because* we are under Jesus' authority that we reject all such practices in our world. The way to avoid such implications is to treat the fantasy world as separate from ours, not making distinction solely on the basis of whether we believe the author to be a "real" Christian.

How to Deal with This Danger

Simply put, do not have anything to do with foolish and stupid arguments.

Practice discretion. Romans 14:22 states, "So whatever you believe about these things keep between yourself and God." Who says we have to declare our position? When asked where you stand on Harry Potter, consider saying, "I believe that's a matter of personal conviction before God. Christians can rightly choose either way."

Aim to be logical and consistent. Decide *what* you object to, then apply any conscientious objections consistently across the board. If you throw out Harry Potter for using such terminology and portrayals of "good magic," you'd have to throw out *The Wizard of Oz,* Greek and Roman mythology, Grimm's Fairy Tales, *Sleeping Beauty, Cinderella, Peter Pan, Pinocchio, Beauty and the Beast, The Sword in the Stone, The Hobbit,* Lord of the Rings, Narnia, and the list goes on and on.

Ask God for wisdom. We need God's wisdom to think these things through. He promises to supply it. Test what you think is God's wisdom by comparing it to the description in James 3:17-18: "The wisdom that comes from heaven is first of all pure; then peace-loving, considerate, submissive, full of mercy and good fruit, impartial and sincere. Peacemakers who sow in peace raise a harvest of righteousness."

The overall danger of the Harry Potter debate is that the body of Christ will become so frustrated, factious, or just plain weary that we never get around to the central issue on which we all agree: Kids need to be protected from real influences of the occult in the real world. That's what we take up next. So whatever your ultimate decision about Harry Potter, I hope you can use the instructions in the next chapter to clearly explain to kids the real dangers of the occult and help them decide to "Have nothing to do with the fruitless deeds of darkness, but rather expose them" (Ephesians 5:11).

CHAPTER SEVEN

PROTECTING KIDS FROM REAL-WORLD OCCULT

*Vital Information and Instruction
Kids Need to Stay Safe*

Merely debating what might happen if kids get the wrong ideas about the occult does nothing to protect them from real dangers. Regardless of the position you may take on Harry Potter, you are a member of the Christian community, which has a more crucial issue at stake: to make sure children are clear on biblical warnings against the occult. The Harry Potter debate stirs curiosity, and kids already have a keen interest in spiritual things. Therefore, let's use their curiosity about Harry Potter to lead them into a clear explanation and understanding of the spiritual realm as revealed in the Bible. We can't assume that Christian kids are clear on this, especially given the confusing mix of occult messages in popular culture.

Magic in literature is used as a way to make the story exciting and expand the possibilities beyond the limits of our real world. In the case of Harry Potter, J. K. Rowling has stated that she does not want kids to emulate the practices of witchcraft and wizardry in our real world. However, intentions don't dictate what kids actually do. Movie, TV, and video game producers do not *intend* violence in their programs and games to cause kids to act violently. Even so, sometimes this risk becomes a reality.

The Harry Potter series has an added element of danger (if you don't understand why Christians are in an uproar, this may help you understand): The author does not believe in real witchcraft or magic. As a result, she treats these elements within her stories as if they do not have real equivalents in our world. But what if there are? And what if these spiritual forces are invisible, malevolent, and deceptive? Where does that leave kids who think they are just playing out what they have read in the story?

In fact, we know that some kids are playing out such things. Rowling has noted that some kids in line at book signings have whispered to her, "We're doing the spells…," to which she replied, in effect, "Don't bother. They're not real. I made them up." So even though the author has not used any real spells or incantations in her novels, we now see kids doing what she never intended: acting out what they've encountered in a fantasy imaginary world.

Here is the *real danger:* Kids think it's "only fantasy." That is all Rowling wrote it to be. She has also stated that she doesn't believe in witchcraft or magic in our world.[1] As a result, she would not see the danger kids might encounter if they act out what they've read. The Bible cautions us to be on guard against invisible forces of spiritual evil. The combination of the author's disbelief, kids' tendency to act out what they encounter in engaging fantasy worlds, and the Bible's warnings forms a triangle of real danger for real kids—even though no one intended it.

Here's why: (1) Kids don't understand that what works in a fantasy story won't work the same way in the real world; (2) this generation has been raised on virtual reality, where it's unclear what is real and what is not; and (3) there are invisible forces at work that influence what can happen to them, even if they don't realize it.

Let me use a real example that is less frightful than the thought of encountering invisible and malevolent forces of spiritual darkness. When I was in kindergarten, I came home from school every day and watched my favorite cartoon, *Felix the Cat.* How harmful could Felix be? "Felix the Cat, Felix the Cat. You'll laugh so hard your sides will ache, your heart will go pitter-pat, watching Felix the wonderful cat!" I still can hear the theme song! Felix was no ordinary cat. He had a magic bag of tricks. Whenever he got into trouble, he opened his magic bag and pulled out a remedy. He could pull out all kinds of powerful abilities. He'd say the magic words, tell the bag what he wanted, and get the power he needed. I had to have one of those bags! So my mom gave me a handbag, and I pretended it was my "bag of tricks." I'd watch, remember the words, and marvel at the power in that magic bag.

I was only five. Obviously, I did not understand the difference between a cartoon fantasy and real life. I believed that if I said the right words, I, too, could pull magic power out of my bag of tricks. So I took my bag, hoisted myself up onto the three-foot block wall around my sister's house, and walked along it, up the graduated levels until I was standing on top—eight feet above the ground. I was so excited! I had my bag of tricks! I had memorized the words! I was ready to fly, completely unafraid. I knew nothing of the invisible force of gravity, but that did not stop it from exerting its power over me the moment I jumped.

I landed hard and bit down on my tongue with such force that it was partially severed. I was rushed to the emergency room, lost a lot of blood, and spent a terrifying night in the hospital. All because (1) I didn't understand that what worked for Felix wouldn't work the same way in my real world, (2) I had an unclear delineation between fantasy and reality, and (3) my lack of understanding about the invisible force of gravity left me without the necessary caution to protect myself.

(I must add a word for any reader who does not believe there are invisible and evil spirit beings seeking to influence and harm unsuspecting people: What if the Bible is absolutely true on this point and you are not? What if God's warnings in the Bible are true? Can you see how people who believe they are would rightfully be alarmed over others telling their kids, "Don't worry. All the witchcraft and questionable practices depicted in the Harry Potter books are *just fantasy.*" What if the practices written as fantasy turn out not to be "just fantasy" when practiced in the real world? This is why Christians are so alarmed. We believe the Bible reveals the truth about that which we cannot see.)

Now a word for Christian parents, church leaders, and concerned adults: I see a blessing for our kids hidden in the popularity of the Harry Potter books. We are being forced to take action with regard to our responsibility to educate and equip our children to resist the devil. Occult themes have become prevalent, even acceptable, in our culture, so exploring these issues with our children doesn't pose any new or added spiritual threat. Rather, we can no longer avoid preparing kids to deal with these spiritual realities. To whatever degree the debate over Harry Potter has spurred us to educate and equip our kids to overcome evil with good, it turns into a blessing! And I praise God for the intense interest that leads parents to pursue their kids' spiritual well-being and protection.

CONCERNED BUT NOT CONFIDENT ABOUT WHAT TO SAY?

No doubt you are concerned about children, but perhaps you are not sure what to teach them, how to go about it, or hesitant that you won't have answers to the questions they raise. This chapter will give you the basics from the Bible that kids need to know to steer clear of the occult in our real world. It is written in kid-speak, so you could just read it to them verbatim. However, I suggest you review it first. Check out all the Scripture verses to make sure you understand them yourself. Perhaps talk with your children's pastor at church, your youth pastor, or even a group of parents willing to discuss these important biblical points so you have a grasp of the material. Also, follow these tips as you share the information with your kids:

- Don't read this to them all at once. These are monumental concepts to a child.

- Read the emotion in their faces and body language. Address any fears or confusion.

- Ask questions to see how they're processing what you say and what conclusions they're drawing. Correct them as necessary.

- Don't focus your attention on demonic powers, Satan, hell, and aspects of darkness. Instead, focus their attention above (see Colossians 3:1-4) on Jesus Christ and all the power of God.

- Share these things with confident assurance that God is greater than all the forces of evil and fully committed to protecting those who take refuge in him. Kids will follow your emotional lead. If you are fearful, you open them up to fear.

- Treat your children's fears respectfully. Reassure them with God's promises that they need not be afraid.

- Realize that these concepts are truly scary to children. Kids have long suspected that there is something terrible lurking in the dark, just waiting and wanting to get them. You're confirming their worst fears, and you must be prepared to put those fears immediately to rest.

- Pray with them and over them to be fully protected from the evil one. Teach them to pray the Lord's Prayer (Matthew 6:9-13) and to memorize verses that give them power over evil (see chapter 8, "Stick to Scripture").

- Answer their questions as they come up. If you don't have an answer, write the question down and take it to someone on your church staff who can help you both find the answer. This will generate more questions than you have answers to, but that's okay. The curiosity will lead you and your child into Bible study and a closer relationship with God.

- Be prepared to lead your child into a personal relationship with Jesus Christ. Once children realize he is their protection, they'll want to enter in. (See chapter 11 for help.)

I hope the following explanation proves helpful to you. Should you need further guidance, contact your local church.

EVERYBODY WANTS POWER

People look for ways to find power and help in real life. That may explain why people love stories with magic. The Bible tells us that God offers people all the power and help needed for all areas of life and all situations.

LOOK TO GOD FOR POWER—
AND EVERYTHING ELSE YOU NEED

We should look to God for the power we need and ask him for help. God hears and answers prayer, although sometimes his answer isn't what we expect. Sometimes God gives people courage and strength to face problems. Sometimes he sends help through the love and support of family, friends, or others who also have faith in God.

Sometimes God sends wisdom, so people can come up with new ways to solve their problems or fill needs. Sometimes God answers prayers in ways that seem ordinary or lucky. When we pray and things just seem to work out, we call this providence. That means God is providing what we need.

God gives people spiritual gifts and natural abilities. Sometimes he provides what we need through those natural abilities. But when God answers prayer in ways that go beyond anything we could do in our own natural abilities, that's called *supernatural.* These supernatural displays of God's power are called signs (because they are meant to point people to God), wonders (because it makes people *wonder* what powerful person or force caused it to happen), or miracles. Sometimes—even today—God works in supernatural ways.

WHERE TO GO FOR SUPERNATURAL POWER

When we need supernatural power, we should turn to God. He is almighty; that means there is no limit to his might and power. God is all-knowing; that means he knows everything. So God should be our ultimate source of knowledge. God is all-wise. Whenever we don't know what to do, are confused, or need wisdom, we should seek God. The Bible promises us that God will give wisdom to all who ask for it without doubting that God will answer (see James 1:5-6). God is all-good. He loves us very much. So we can trust God and be sure what he commands is best for us. God wants us to know him so his power and wisdom can work in and through us.

ONE *HUGE* WARNING!

God gives us one *huge* warning: We must not seek any supernatural power or spiritual help from any source other than him! God sees everything, even things going on that are invisible to humans. In the Bible, God reveals things going on in the invisible spiritual world that influence our physical world.

AN INVISIBLE BATTLE

The Bible tells us that spiritual beings, both good and evil, work behind the scenes to influence people. The spirits try to influence our understanding of God, nature, and life. The evil ones do this to get people to believe things that will lead them away from the one true God. Evil ones always use many tricks to keep people distracted from God, because they know that people who do not trust Jesus Christ in this life will be doomed for eternity. Some false beliefs, other religions, and even talk about "spiritual sources" can sound good. But if these things do not lead us to trust Jesus Christ, they leave us unprotected from evil influences. Evil spirits may even promise good things, but they really want people's souls to be destroyed forever.

These evil spirits all started out as God's holy angels. But they rebelled against God by following an angel who wanted to be greater than God. His name is Lucifer. We also call him Satan, the devil, the accuser, or the evil one. God threw Satan and his followers (the evil spirits, or demons) out of heaven. Jesus saw this and described it for us. Jesus told his disciples, "I saw Satan fall like lightning from heaven. I have given you authority to trample on snakes and scorpions and to overcome all the power of the enemy; nothing will harm you. However, do not rejoice that the spirits submit to you, but rejoice that your names are written in heaven" (Luke 10:18-20).

Ever since Satan was thrown out of heaven, people have lived in the middle of a spiritual battle. God and those loyal to him battle Satan and his demons for the souls of people. God loves people. He wants them to be in his kingdom and experience all the glories of heaven forever and ever. Satan knows how much God loves people, so destroying them is his way of getting back at God. Satan tries to trick people into rebelling against God. He knows if they do, they will be destroyed right along with him.

GOD AND SATAN FIGHT ON OPPOSITE SIDES, BUT THEY'RE NOT EQUALS

God is the Creator. Satan and all the demons were created by God. They are powerful, but they don't even come close to having the kind of power God Almighty has. There is a lot that we don't fully understand about what goes on in the invisible spiritual world. That is why we always need to obey God.

Because God loves us and knows everything that goes on, even spiritual things, he is able to guide us safely.

IT IS POSSIBLE TO MAKE CONTACT WITH SPIRIT BEINGS, BUT WATCH OUT!

The Bible says it is possible for people to make contact with this invisible spiritual world. We saw this when Jesus, his disciples, and others commanded demons to get out of people, and the demons had to obey. We saw it in the Old Testament when a witch or medium called up the spirit of Samuel and he came. We also know this is possible, otherwise God wouldn't tell us not to do it! And the apostle Paul said people who worship idols actually contact demons. God's Word acknowledges that spirit beings have some level of knowledge, power, and influence. Some people seek out evil spiritual forces for power, help, or to get secret knowledge. But God *forbids* people to make contact with any spiritual being that is not on God's side. The spiritual forces and beings on Satan's side are dangerous and tricky! Any time people contact spiritual forces *not* on God's side, their actions are called "occult."

GOD'S HOLY SPIRIT AND ANGELS HELP US

God sent his own Holy Spirit to help his people in special ways (see John 14–17). His holy angels can also bring messages or assistance. Hebrews 13:2 says, "Do not forget to entertain strangers, for by so doing some people have entertained angels without knowing it." It seems that children have special protection from angels. Jesus said: "See that you do not look down on one of these little ones. For I tell you that their angels in heaven always see the face of my Father in heaven" (Matthew 18:10). We can thank God for his holy angels and the work they do that we may not know about.

But we should never worship angels. They, too, are creations of God that serve him. Also, remember there are twice as many angels on God's side. Only one-third of the angels rebelled; two-thirds remained loyal to God. So we have double the forces!

THE BIBLE GIVES US A LIST OF SPIRITUAL THINGS WE SHOULD *NEVER* DO

In Deuteronomy 18:9-14 is God's list of things we must NEVER try or dabble in. (Remember, evil spirits may try to trick you into thinking they are good. If they are really on God's side, they will obey God's Word. Therefore, any spirit leading you to do any of these forbidden things is *not* on God's side!)

Parents, *Never* Offer Your Children As a Human Sacrifice

I'm sure kids are glad God put that one in there! Some people actually have given their children as sacrifices to demons or idols. They would kill their children or put them in the arms of an idol called Baal and burn them to death! Remember that the spirits behind the activities on the rest of this list are just as murderous. That's why God warns us—for our own protection!

Never Practice Divination

Divination is the practice of fortune-telling. God knows what our future holds. If we need to know, he'll let us know. Bible prophecies foretell important events before they happen. God did this so people would know that he alone is God (see Isaiah 44). Evil spirits try to copy this by giving some people (such as psychics, fortune-tellers, palm readers, astrologers) power to tell the future in a limited and imperfect way. Astrologers read meaning from the patterns of the stars and write horoscopes based on what they see. In the Bible, God sometimes fulfilled prophecies by using the heavens— like when he announced Christ's birth with the Christmas star—but astrology and horoscopes try to reveal the future apart from God. That kind of divination is forbidden, because there are evil spiritual forces behind them (even though many people don't know or believe this). These spiritual forces want to control people.

The people who try to know the future apart from God might even be taken over by an evil spirit they cannot control. The Bible tells about an encounter Jesus' followers had with a girl controlled by such a spirit. Luke wrote in Acts 16:16-19:

> Once when we were going to the place of prayer, we were met by a slave girl who had a spirit by which she predicted the future. She earned a great deal of money for her owners by fortune-telling. This girl followed Paul and the rest of us, shouting, "These men are servants of the Most High God, who are telling you the way to be saved." She kept this up for many days. Finally Paul became so troubled that he turned around and said to the spirit, "In the name of Jesus Christ I command you to come out of her!" At that moment the spirit left her. When the owners of the slave girl realized that their hope of making money was gone, they seized Paul and Silas and dragged them into the marketplace to face the authorities.

This girl was controlled by a demon—not God's Holy Spirit—that gave her the ability to tell the future. She was held as a slave and used to make money for her owners with her ability to practice divination. The Bible doesn't deny that this was real. God's servants forced the spirit out of her in the authority of Jesus.

Spirits don't die like people do. The same spirits who could tell the future then continue to do so today. *Never* try any thing that promises to tell the future. It may be fake, or it might open you up to real, dangerous spirit beings God wants to protect you from. Common forms of divination include using a Ouija board (it's more than a game!), consulting psychics, reading tarot cards, or using a crystal ball.

Never Practice Sorcery or Try to Use Magic Powers

People want power! Most fantasy stories have a showdown between good and evil to see who is most powerful. If good wins, they do good. If evil wins, they kill and destroy. Humans have power, like intelligence, political power, or the power of working together. This power can be used for good or evil. God wants people to use their power for good. There is also supernatural power from spiritual sources. The Bible has many showdowns where the good battle evil with supernatural power: Elijah versus the prophets of Baal (1 Kings 18); Aaron and Moses versus Egyptian magicians (Exodus 7); Jesus versus Satan (Matthew 4), and Paul versus Elymas the sorcerer (Acts 13).

These Bible accounts show that sorcerers can have real power. That doesn't mean they're good. Jesus warned, "False Christs and false prophets will appear and perform great signs and miracles to deceive even the elect— if that were possible. See, I have told you ahead of time" (Matthew 24:24-25). Some who claim this kind of power are fakes, but some use real spiritual power that is not from God. Some "magicians" only create illusions. Their tricks are amazing, but because these entertainers don't contact spiritual forces, the illusions are not occult. This "magic" includes things like pulling a rabbit out of a hat, card tricks, and making something disappear.

Never Interpret Omens to Discover Hidden Knowledge

Throughout history people often looked for signs in nature, such as in weather or in the appearance of a certain animal or bird. Ancient Romans considered the sight of a crow a "bad omen" that predicted death or tragedy. Interpreting omens is associated with superstitions. Reading tea leaves or being afraid of black cats fall into this category.

God doesn't want superstition, omens, or other natural signs to control us by fear. We belong to a loving God who takes care of us no matter what. The Bible shows how God warned people of danger in dreams. He also sent prophets, who told people to change their ways to prevent bad things. When we look to omens, we're not trusting God. Besides, you could be misled or ruled by fear if every "omen" made you think something terrible was about to happen. God doesn't want us to live in fear of the future.

Never Cast Spells!

Some people cast spells to protect themselves from danger or inflict harm on an enemy. Casting spells or reciting incantations involves repeating words or saying mysterious phrases. You may think you're just playing around, or you may be trying to make something good happen, but you might really be calling on evil spiritual forces to do what you want.

When people call upon spirits, even if they don't really believe in them or know their names, there's a chance the spirits may actually come! When this happens, you may find yourself under the influence of a spiritual force you can't possibly handle. Besides, casting a spell is a poor substitute for the real power and access to help that is offered to us by God. God has offered us the privilege of prayer. We don't have to mutter phrases in hopes of stirring up some kind of cosmic force (that really wants to hurt us). God invites us to come to him; we have access to God himself. The Bible says, "Let us then approach the throne of grace with confidence, so that we may receive mercy and find grace to help us in our time of need" (Hebrews 4:16). That's quite an invitation!

The Bible is like a collection of God's love letters to us. In it, he gives us many promises that offer us ways to influence our world. Jesus Christ came to earth to meet us here and offer us the kingdom and power of God. When we pray in Jesus' name and authority we have assurance that God hears us. We don't need to cast spells. We have a better option. Jesus contrasted muttering a spell, or "babbling," with how his followers should pray. He said:

> And when you pray, do not keep on babbling like pagans, for they think they will be heard because of their many words. Do not be like them, for your Father knows what you need before you ask him.
>
> This, then, is how you should pray:

"Our Father in heaven,

hallowed be your name,

your kingdom come,

your will be done

on earth as it is in heaven.

Give us today our daily bread.

Forgive us our debts,

as we also have forgiven our debtors.

And lead us not into temptation,

but deliver us from the evil one" (Matthew 6:7-13).

Instead of looking at a book of spells, incantations, or anything like that, remember that you have a personal relationship with the living God. (Or if you don't yet, you *can.* See chapter 11 to learn how.) Even though God created the universe and holds it all together by his almighty power, he's available to you. Not only that, this *awesome* God knows that you have needs, cares about your needs, and gives you this pattern to follow to bring all your needs to him. You don't have to say just the right words! You don't have to do any fancy motions! All you have to do is speak from your heart, to God, and God will hear your prayers, guide you into his will for your life, help you, and meet your needs.

Never Consult a Medium or Spiritist, and *Never* Offer Yourself As a Medium Through Which a Spirit or Spirits Could Communicate to Others

A medium or spiritist is a person who lets a spirit or spirits come into them. Sometimes they let the spirits speak through them. Some people advertise this as a service to others! They may sincerely believe they are using a special gift to help people gain access to the spirit world. They may offer their customers access to communicate with the spirit of a dead loved one or someone else who lived at another time in history. When people get

138

together to try to contact spirits, this is called a séance. This can be a meeting where the person who regularly serves as a medium opens up to spirits and "channels" messages from the spirit world to people in our world.

All of these methods are basically the same thing: A human being created by God to be filled with his Holy Spirit serves other spirits instead. But God created us to be united with him and filled with *his* Spirit. That's why you may feel a deep longing for something supernatural or for contact with the spiritual world. If we respond to that desire by opening ourselves to spirits that are not of God, it's like being unfaithful to him. God wants us to offer our bodies to him (see Romans 12:1-2) so his Spirit can fill us and flow through us to the world. If we refuse to have this relationship with God, we grieve God and hurt ourselves. God also gets angry when people choose other spirits. Think of how parents get angry if their child hangs out with a group known to cause trouble. Why are they angry? Because they love their child. They know that their son or daughter is in danger. God knows that evil spiritual forces are a danger to you.

As if that weren't enough, the Bible gives other good reasons for not consulting mediums and spiritists. The prophet Isaiah wrote, "When men tell you to consult mediums and spiritists, who whisper and mutter, should not a people inquire of their God? Why consult the dead on behalf of the living? To the law and to the testimony! If they do not speak according to this word, they have no light of dawn" (Isaiah 8:19-20).

When the prophet says "to the law and to the testimony," he is talking about the truth of God revealed in the Old Testament. When he says "they have no light," it means people can't see this truth clearly. God sees everything—even in the dark. When people consult mediums or spiritists, they contact spirits of darkness.

God is truthful. Demonic spirits are deceitful. The prophet Jeremiah said, "They prophesy lies" (Jeremiah 27:10). You can tell whether a spirit is from God by testing to see if it agrees with what God reveals in the Bible. In this case it was the Old Testament "law and testimonies."

After Jesus came, we were given another test of whether a spirit is God's Holy Spirit. The apostle John wrote, "This is how you can recognize the Spirit of God: Every spirit that acknowledges that Jesus Christ has come in the flesh is from God, but every spirit that does not acknowledge Jesus is not from God. This is the spirit of the antichrist, which you have heard is coming and even now is already in the world" (1 John 4:2-3).

Finally, turning to mediums and spiritists can break your fellowship with God. When the people of the nation of Israel turned to them, God said, "I will set my face against the person who turns to mediums and spiritists to prostitute himself by following them, and I will cut him off from his people" (Leviticus 20:6).

Never Try to Consult the Dead!

People sometimes try to contact spirits of the dead, or ghosts. They may think this is a fun game, but it is very dangerous. If you are ever invited to be part of a séance, *don't*—even if your friends say they're just playing around. You could get what you ask for and unexpected dangers besides, including demon possession.

Jesus Christ has authority over all spirits. Demons have to obey his commands. When Jesus lived on earth, people brought those who were demon possessed to Jesus for relief. We can read such an account in Mark 9:17-29:

> A man in the crowd answered, "Teacher, I brought you my son, who is possessed by a spirit that has robbed him of speech. Whenever it seizes him, it throws him to the ground. He foams at the mouth, gnashes his teeth and becomes rigid. I asked your disciples to drive out the spirit, but they could not."
>
> "O unbelieving generation," Jesus replied, "how long shall I stay with you? How long shall I put up with you? Bring the boy to me."

So they brought him. When the spirit saw Jesus, it immediately threw the boy into a convulsion. He fell to the ground and rolled around, foaming at the mouth.

Jesus asked the boy's father, "How long has he been like this?"

"From childhood," he answered. "It has often thrown him into fire or water to kill him. But if you can do anything, take pity on us and help us."

" 'If you can'?" said Jesus. "Everything is possible for him who believes."

Immediately the boy's father exclaimed, "I do believe; help me overcome my unbelief!"

When Jesus saw that a crowd was running to the scene, he rebuked the evil spirit. "You deaf and mute spirit," he said, "I command you, come out of him and never enter him again."

The spirit shrieked, convulsed him violently and came out. The boy looked so much like a corpse that many said, "He's dead." But Jesus took him by the hand and lifted him to his feet, and he stood up.

After Jesus had gone indoors, his disciples asked him privately, "Why couldn't we drive it out?"

He replied, "This kind can come out only by prayer."

When we trust Jesus and obey God by not trying to contact ghosts or other spirits, he will protect us. Those who disobey these warnings enter into real danger.

Even people who believe in God have turned to spirits of the dead. The results are disastrous! Saul, a king appointed by God, decided to try to consult the dead prophet Samuel, even though he had made a law against consulting the dead through a medium! That story can be found in 1 Samuel 28 and 31. (Parents, I recommend you read this first and paraphrase. The gore in this story is more graphic than anything in Harry Potter.) It's *not* a pretty story. Saul was not ready for the message he got when the medium contacted Samuel in the afterlife. Samuel's spirit brought a message from God to Saul: Saul's disobedience would lead to his death. Samuel told Saul in great detail how he and his sons were going to die—the very next day.

First Chronicles 10:13-14 says, "Saul died because he was unfaithful to the LORD; he did not keep the word of the LORD and even consulted a medium for guidance, and did not inquire of the LORD. So the LORD put him to death and turned the kingdom over to David son of Jesse." This is a sad and troubling account of someone who once looked to God for guidance, and was blessed; then he turned away from God and came to a terrible end.

One more thing: When people try to contact the dead, they may think they're talking to the spirit of a dearly departed loved one, but they might really be talking to a spirit *pretending* to be that loved one. These are called familiar spirits, because they are familiar with people who have lived before. A demonic spirit can influence people in this world by pretending to be someone who lived before.

Never Engage in Witchcraft

This term includes any appeal to occult powers—*any* supernatural power or spirit other than God, the Holy Spirit.

Wicca is a modern-day pagan religion that practices witchcraft and worships nature and goddesses. Some say this kind of witchcraft is good and deny its involvement with demonic powers or Satan. That's not what God says.

Christians must shun all worship of any deity other than the one true God revealed in the Bible. Not only that, God says that all contact with witchcraft, all worship of other "so-called" gods and goddesses or the worship of nature is idolatry. Idolatry and witchcraft go together, and both are *forbidden*. Even those who claim to practice "white witchcraft" or "good magic" will admit that they worship nature and goddesses. That alone is enough to qualify Wicca as strictly forbidden by God. Even people who think they are practicing a religion free from satanic influence may be deceived. The apostle Paul wrote, "Satan himself masquerades as an angel of light. It is not surprising, then, if his servants masquerade as servants of righteousness. Their end will be what their actions deserve" (2 Corinthians 11:14-15).

Witchcraft is also associated with the use of drugs. One of the words used to describe witchcraft in Revelation 21:8 and 22:15 is the Greek word *pharmakos*. A similar word *pharmakia* is translated as sorcery or witchcraft in Galatians 5:20. Some people use spells, enchantments, and calling on spirits to try to exert power. Some people use drugs and potions while calling on spiritual forces to try to make something happen. Vine's *Expository Dictionary of New Testament Words* explains: "In sorcery, the use of drugs, whether simple or potent, was generally accompanied by incantations and appeals to occult powers, with the provision of various charms, amulets, etc., and professedly designed to keep the applicant or patient from the attention and power of demons, but actually to impress the applicant with the mysterious resources and powers of the sorcerer."[2] So don't try any spells, incantations, or potions, and don't use mind-altering drugs. That might alter more than your mood.

Many products sold today cross the line from pretend play into witchcraft. With all the interest in Harry Potter, some companies are selling books full of spells, "wizard kits," incantations, recipes for potions, "magic charms," amulets (which are like a good-luck charm), talismans (a piece of jewelry that is supposed to ward off evil spirits), and so on. Don't rely on any object to ward off evil. You don't need a "lucky charm" when you are depending on the living God.

TURN ALL YOUR INTEREST IN SPIRITUAL THINGS TOWARD GOD

People can be overwhelmed by the many details they encounter when trying to learn about the supernatural world. Even Christians can get so focused on learning about evil spirits that they end up afraid or more focused on the devil than on God. That's not good! When you feel interested in spiritual things, even supernatural things, turn that interest toward God. That's the ultimate source of supernatural power and influence. Commit yourself to seek help, protection, and power *from God only.*

All of these commands are given to us for our protection. Make sure you fully understand these boundaries set by God. Make up your own mind *never* to practice any of these things. Also, warn your friends.

As people get excited about the Harry Potter fantasy stories, some kids may get confused and think that what is cool in Harry Potter's fantasy world would be cool to try in our world. J. K. Rowling has made it clear that she never intended that. So let the "magic" of Harry Potter's world stay in the realm of fantasy. In the real world, the way to look for supernatural power is to seek God and his kingdom.

One more note about fantasy stories: In children's literature, the use of "magic wands," spells, enchantments, and so on are common, even in books written by Christians. Sometimes a storyteller will use practices like gazing into a crystal ball, reading tea leaves, or casting a spell. Those things may make the story more exciting, but that does not mean we should practice those things ourselves. The Bible clearly forbids us from doing so.

Also, some stories have characters that are good witches, wizards, and magicians, such as Glenda the "Good Witch" in *The Wizard of Oz,* Professors McGonogall and Dumbledore in Harry Potter, the wizard Gandalf in *The Hobbit,* or the "good magician" Coriakin in *Prince Caspian* (Narnia). In a fantasy story where there is a battle between good and evil, the author may use a "good witch" (like Glenda) to fight evil (like the Wicked Witch of the West). Don't take this literary device to mean that there can be "good witches" or "good witchcraft" in our real world. In fantasy, a good-witch-versus-bad-witch plot can be used symbolically to make the story work. In our world, we go by what God reveals to us in the Bible. And God's Word makes it clear that *in real life* there is no such thing as good witchcraft!

CHAPTER EIGHT

BE *IN* THE WORLD BUT NOT *OF* THE WORLD

Engaging in Our Culture Without Disobeying God

"Let those who love the LORD hate evil" (Psalm 97:10). Those of us who love the Lord and love our children not only hate evil, we try to do all we can to protect our kids from evil. The Bible makes it clear that this includes protecting them from spiritual forces of wickedness. We are also charged with helping our children learn to guard their hearts and minds from the deceptive and destructive forces of evil, which often masquerade as harmless, or even good, forces.

Protecting children can be quite a challenge, given how our culture barrages them daily with a myriad of occult influences. Surf the television networks and you'll find family-hour offerings such as *Sabrina, the Teenage Witch; Charmed;* and *Buffy the Vampire Slayer.* TV commercials advertise the services of psychics and tarot card readers. Kids openly tell tales of playing with Ouija boards, levitating someone at slumber parties, or making contact with "spirit guides." Beads, charms, or crystals that promise to bring the wearer peace, happiness, and prosperity are the height of fashion. While browsing a mega-bookstore, my son spotted a display case filled with fortune-telling paraphernalia. It seems that paganism, witchcraft, and all manner of occult references permeate the world we live in. Although these kinds of influences have always existed, our culture seems to be embracing such activities now as acceptable or even good.

When my husband, Patrick, and I took on this subject for consideration, we called a family meeting. We invited our children (ages nine, ten, and fifteen) to join in the discussion by reporting where they saw occult influences in their everyday lives. In less than ten minutes, they came up with a list of over thirty TV shows and movies that featured some use of occult powers. They listed several ways in which they were confronted by such references with friends, at school, at the mall, and even on the radio. Our family was quickly convinced that we couldn't avoid occult influences without completely separating ourselves from our culture. For us, that isn't an option because we are committed to fulfill Jesus' command to *"Go into all the world"* with the good news of God's love. Somehow, we have to help our kids be in the world but not of the world.

I understand why many Christians, especially parents and grandparents, are deeply concerned about entertainment that presents witchcraft, wizardry, and divination in any kind of positive light. Some deem Harry Potter the Joe Camel of our paganized culture. I understand why some Christians choose to forbid and guard against the stories; that is the right decision for them (see chapter 5). My husband and I, however, checked with the Lord, researched the matter, and felt released to read the books. As a parent, Bible teacher, and volunteer youth leader, I felt I needed to understand their appeal so that I could make informed decisions about how to protect my kids from any influence of evil. After I previewed the first book, Patrick and I considered our children and decided to read the series aloud with our entire family.

While reading the Harry Potter books will not be the right decision for all Christian families, I would like you to consider a biblically viable alternative to simply forbidding these stories.

DANIEL: A MODEL FOR OUR TIMES

My first stop when examining almost any issue is to do a thorough check of the Bible to consider all references to it. On the Harry Potter issues, I used a computer program to search the Bible for every reference to magicians, sorcerers, witchcraft, wizardry, and a few other associated terms. In Daniel 4:9 I found a startling entry that challenged my initial line of reasoning on this issue: "I said, 'Belteshazzar, chief of the magicians, I know that the spirit of the holy gods is in you, and no mystery is too difficult for you. Here is my dream; interpret it for me.'"

Who is Belteshazzar? According to Daniel 1:7, "The chief official gave them new names: to Daniel, the name Belteshazzar." The Jewish exiles were even given new names in honor of Babylonian gods. Belteshazzar means "Lord Marduke [a Babylonian deity] protect his life." The Bible tells us that King Nebuchadnezzar gave the prophet Daniel the title "chief of the magicians."

One of Nebuchadnezzar's descendants got himself into trouble by drinking out of the sacred vessels brought to Babylon from God's temple in Jerusalem. A human hand appeared and wrote a mysterious message on the wall, and no one could interpret it. Then the mother of the king said to her son: "There is a man in your kingdom who has the spirit of the holy gods in him. In the time of your father he was found to have insight and intelligence and wisdom like that of the gods. King Nebuchadnezzar your father—your father the king, I say—appointed him chief of the magicians, enchanters, astrologers and diviners. This man Daniel, whom the king called Belteshazzar…" (Daniel 5:11-12).

The biblical hero, *Daniel?* Chief of the magicians, enchanters, astrologers, and diviners? How could this be?

Few Christians would ever dare describe the prophet Daniel as such. He was the holy prophet who dared to face a den full of ravenous lions rather than cease praying to the only true God three times a day. He was the one whose close friends were thrown into the fiery furnace rather than bow to an idol. As a teen, Daniel was taken captive when the Babylonians conquered Judah. Daniel and his God-fearing friends were taken by force into a foreign culture, where they risked execution rather than defile themselves with the king's rich foods that violated Jewish dietary laws. Although forced to live in Babylon, all of them refused to disobey God, even when threatened with death.

Surely *that* Daniel never practiced these forbidden practices! That's right—he never practiced occult magic because he never called on their gods, even though they called him by the name of one of their gods.

Daniel and his God-worshiping friends were chosen to learn the language and literature of the Babylonians (Daniel 1:4). He was trained alongside the "magicians" and "seers" who worked for the King. There is no indication that Daniel and friends refused to hear or read the literature. In fact when tested on what they learned, they surpassed their peers (1:19). However, they drew the line when it came to violating God's laws. They did not call on any spiritual force other than the one true God or disrupt their personal devotion to God. They lived in and attended a three-year school with the magicians, seers, and astrologers of Babylon, where the students were trained in language, literature, and magical arts (or science and wisdom of the times).

Daniel and his three friends were "in the world" about as far as anyone can be, and yet Daniel "resolved not to defile himself" (1:8). He refused the king's foods, which were restricted by Jewish dietary laws. He stood firm and resisted the forces of evil all around and was used to show how superior God's power is to all occult powers.

One night the king had a troubling dream. He demanded that one of his magicians interpret the dream—without him telling them its contents! He required them to describe the dream to him so he would know they weren't just making up an interpretation. I'll let Daniel 2:10-28 tell the rest of the story:

> The astrologers answered the king, "There is not a man on earth who can do what the king asks! No king, however great and mighty, has ever asked such a thing of any magician or enchanter or astrologer. What the king asks is too difficult. No one can reveal it to the king except the gods, and they do not live among men."

This made the king so angry and furious that he ordered the execution of all the wise men of Babylon. So the decree was issued to put the wise men to death, and men were sent to look for Daniel and his friends to put them to death.

When Arioch, the commander of the king's guard, had gone out to put to death the wise men of Babylon, Daniel spoke to him with wisdom and tact. He asked the king's officer, "Why did the king issue such a harsh decree?" Arioch then explained the matter to Daniel. At this, Daniel went in to the king and asked for time, so that he might interpret the dream for him.

Then Daniel returned to his house and explained the matter to his friends Hananiah, Mishael and Azariah. [Also known as Shadrach, Meshach, and Abednego.] He urged them to plead for mercy from the God of heaven concerning this mystery, so that he and his friends might not be executed with the rest of the wise men of Babylon. During the night the mystery was revealed to Daniel in a vision. Then Daniel praised the God of heaven and said:

"Praise be to the name of God for ever and ever;
    wisdom and power are his.
He changes times and seasons;
    he sets up kings and deposes them.
He gives wisdom to the wise
    and knowledge to the discerning.
He reveals deep and hidden things;
    he knows what lies in darkness,
    and light dwells with him.
I thank and praise you, O God of my fathers:
    You have given me wisdom and power,
you have made known to me what we asked of you,
    you have made known to us the dream of the king."

Then Daniel went to Arioch, whom the king had appointed to execute the wise men of Babylon, and said to him, "Do not execute the wise men of Babylon. Take me to the king, and I will interpret his dream for him."

Arioch took Daniel to the king at once and said, "I have found a man among the exiles from Judah who can tell the king what his dream means."

The king asked Daniel (also called Belteshazzar), "Are you able to tell me what I saw in my dream and interpret it?"

Daniel replied, "No wise man, enchanter, magician or diviner can explain to the king the mystery he has asked about, but there is a God in heaven who reveals mysteries. He has shown King Nebuchadnezzar what will happen in days to come. Your dream and the visions that passed through your mind as you lay on your bed are these:…"

Then he went on to do what no occult practitioner could do, to the glory of God! While surrounded by such forbidden practices, even reading and learning their literature, Daniel never invoked any other spiritual source of power than God. He knew about these things in great detail, but never defiled himself by *practicing* them. Instead he maintained an intimate relationship with God Almighty, whom he called on—to the amazement of all—several times during his life. As a result, proclamations were made by kings and sent throughout the kingdom honoring the God of Daniel.

I found Daniel to be a worthy role model for my children to follow. He lived in a pagan world steeped in the occult. He saw and learned about their occult practices but never joined in and always maintained his belief in the Holy One of Israel. Daniel and his friends were not afraid to read literature that resounded in the hearts of the people with whom they lived. The cultural appetite for the supernatural showed the people's deep need and desire for true supernatural power. Daniel used his familiarity with this pagan culture to prepare him to reveal the true living God to his culture.

Build a Wall or Fit Them with Armor?

So how do we as concerned adults protect our kids from the dangers of the occult that permeate our culture? I do not believe it is biblically viable for parents to ignore the cultural influences facing their children or to abdicate responsibility to train our kids to deal with culture in a godly way. In general, we can take one of two approaches to protect our children from dangerous influences:

- We can try to build a barrier to keep the world out, or…
- We can fit them with armor so they can go into all the world protected against evil influences.

The Downside of Building a Wall

Building a barrier is an attempt to restrict dangerous influences by setting up external limits to keep out anything potentially dangerous—sort of like the great wall of China. Although perhaps more appealing than suiting up for battle, there are many problems with this approach:

- Restricting freedom can incite curiosity and rebellion, leading the one you're trying to protect to try to get past the protective barrier to see what he or she is missing.
- Outside threats are so numerous it is impossible to keep out everything that's potentially harmful. Even if you could keep children separated from all potentially dangerous influences, you would also be keeping them from situations in which they could develop the maturity to ward off such dangers for themselves. By way of practical example, one family worried that their teenage daughter would be in danger if she drove on the freeway. Throughout high school,

they allowed her to drive only on side roads. When she went off to college in a big city, she had to get on the freeway. However, her lack of experience and the fear she had of the real danger combined to send her into hysterics. She managed to pull the car over to the shoulder, but at great personal risk.

- Building a wall assumes that all evil and danger comes from external forces. It disregards the fact that evil also comes from within: "Each one is tempted when, by his own evil desire, he is dragged away and enticed" (James 1:14).

Why Equip Kids to Go Out?

When the Bible gets right down to telling us how to fend off "the devil's schemes" and stand firm against "spiritual forces of darkness in the heavenly realms," it says to put on spiritual armor. This is described in Paul's letter to the Ephesians (6:11-18). The idea of fitting children with spiritual armor represents us helping them develop a personal protection system with which they guard their own hearts and minds. It doesn't mean keeping them from interacting with their culture, even though there are many dangers in it. It means we must equip them to go out into the world, protected at the point of contact with their culture.

Proverbs 4 gives advice to keep young people safe in a dangerous world. Verse 23 says, "Above all else, guard your heart, for it is the wellspring of life." If we can motivate our kids to do this, they will be better able to develop their own spiritual protection system and work with you to fend off the forces of evil. Along the way, they will mature and learn to face life successfully without your continual monitoring.

We're supposed to help our children mature so they can successfully manage life and fend off forces of darkness, which they're bound to encounter in this dark world. The Bible defines those who are mature as those "who because of practice have their senses trained to discern good and evil" (Hebrews 5:14, NASB). So an important part of raising kids is finding ways for them to practice training their senses to discern good and evil. Some of the best practice for developing such discernment, in my opinion, comes by way of using fictional stories and characters.

Stories from popular culture, fiction, and fantasy can be a means of teaching such lessons. This approach is a biblical option, because the restrictions God puts on us in regard to occult involvement are clear-cut (see chapter 7 and Deuteronomy 18:9-16). Daniel's example shows that it is possible for some believers to be educated in the stories of popular culture without violating God's commands.

Fictional situations and characters can be used as a safe, simulated environment in which to define the real dangers of the occult and sort the good from the evil. I never understood the Poke'mon fad or felt comfortable with it. My husband took over researching that one and setting limits for our kids. I questioned my son Taylor about the "psychic" cards. He said, "Mom, don't worry. Dad told us. We know psychics are evil." He pointed out the icon that designated the "psychic" characters and said, "You see these? These do a lot of damage in a battle. We know they are evil, so we sorted them out of our decks. See, we really are learning to sort out good from evil. Besides, when I remember that the psychic Poke'mon cards are the ones that do a lot of damage, that reminds me real psychics do a lot of damage too." I'm not endorsing Poke'mon, just showing how a questionable fad from pop culture was turned into an object lesson.

If you read or view stories from popular culture with your kids, you have the chance to put those stories in a Christian context. You can do as we did with the Harry Potter stories and explain forbidden occult practices while using the stories as illustrations. You can point out the peril and folly involved in real occult practices. You can also note good moral lessons and mistakes the characters make, along with the consequences—all this while helping your children practice discernment skills in a culturally relevant way, showing your kids how to stay in touch with the culture of their peers without doing things God forbids.

How to Protect Kids from Spiritual Forces of Evil

The following strategies have helped our family as we help our kids discern spiritual truth and filter popular culture through Scripture. I hope they will be helpful for your family too.

Go with Your Children

Instead of running from popular culture or leaving children to interpret it on their own, study it and engage in it *with them*. First, preview all questionable materials. My younger kids know that *anything* with occult references has to be previewed and okayed by Patrick and me, whether it's a video game, cartoon, book, or movie. We allow our teenage daughter more personal discretion because she has been demonstrating wisdom in her choices. As you preview, weigh the usefulness of the material. Some may object to anything evil in a story, but the fight between good and evil is often what makes a story useful. Make sure those on the side of good practice virtues such as courage, perseverance, compassion, honesty, loyalty, friendship, self-sacrifice, faith, generosity, and love. Characters don't have to get everything right, but they must realize their errors. Also consider whether the characters on the side of good are called to account when they err, and look for evidence that their consciences are working. Believable characters show human frailty. Look to see how they deal with their errors and wrongdoings and whether their response to it is useful in moral instruction.

Watch for evil that isn't obvious. The Bible says Satan masquerades as an angel of light. The most useful evil characters are those who act friendly but use deception to destroy the good guys. This paints a true picture of how evil works! The villains in Harry Potter are a great example of this.

Whenever evil is shown as scheming, deceptive, selfish, and ultimately destructive, make a lesson of it. We have to help our kids learn how to judge things from a Christian perspective. Sometimes this can mean identifying what's wrong and pointing out bad examples as well as good.

After previewing, and if the Lord allows, read the books, watch the movies, or engage in the activities *with* your children. I never would have let my kids read the Harry Potter books on their own. They needed guidance to be able to put the stories' occult references into a proper context. I told them, "I'll read it with you, but only if we discuss it in light of the Bible." They were eager to do both. If your kids have already read the books on their own, read and discuss each book in light of Scripture as you catch up. Or read aloud and discuss as a family.

As the remaining books come out, I will preread each one to determine whether it's suitable for my children—each considered individually. Judge for yourself; don't rely on someone else (not even me) to tell you what's best for your children. God gave you responsibility for your children's spiritual upbringing. When you engage the culture alongside them, you can use it to teach them to discern whether practices, choices, and characters are good, evil, and/or potentially dangerous.

Stick to Scripture

God's Word, the Bible, is our point of reference for right and wrong. Teach your children to use it—and *how* to use it—whenever they are trying to figure out whether something is permissible. Along with rules of conduct, teach them about the grace of God. Let them know also, "If we claim to be without sin, we deceive ourselves and the truth is not in us. If we confess our sins, he is faithful and just and will forgive us our sins and purify us from all unrighteousness. If we claim we have not sinned, we make him out to be a liar and his word has no place in our lives" (1 John 1:8-10). Remind your children that God gives each of us a free will, and if we choose to disobey God's warnings, which are designed to protect us, there will be consequences.

Also, teach them the Bible passages that show them how to fight and win spiritual battles. It is not unusual for kids to get scared when they realize the reality of spiritual battles. Make sure they are not overcome by fear by keeping the conversation open and giving them the means to win in spiritual battles. Share the following truths with them:

We are on the winning side in this battle against evil! But every person has to do his or her part to overcome evil with good. God has given us three spiritual weapons (see Ephesians 6:10-18). We can use these whenever we feel afraid, sense danger, or see the influence of evil in our lives or the lives of others:

1. Shield of faith (believing God's Word)—Believe God's Word and his promises!
2. Sword of the Spirit (which is the Word of God)—Quote Bible verses out loud!
3. Prayer to God in Jesus' name—Pray to ask God for the help you need! Also memorize the Lord's Prayer found in Matthew 6:9-13 and pray it every day.

Luke 4 tells us of the face-off between Jesus and the devil. Three times Jesus defeated Satan. How? Jesus always believed God's Word, he had spent time in prayer, and he quoted Scripture! Then the devil had to leave him, and good angels came to care for him! You, too, can learn God's promises, believe them, pray to God, and memorize Bible verses. Quote these whenever you are afraid or think you may be dealing with spiritual influences that are opposed to God. Memorize these Bible verses so you're ready:

- "Submit yourselves, then, to God. Resist the devil, and he will flee from you" (James 4:7).
- "But the Lord is faithful, and he will strengthen and protect you from the evil one" (2 Thessalonians 3:3).

- Jesus promised, "Here I am! I stand at the door and knock. If anyone hears my voice and opens the door, I will come in and eat with him, and he with me" (Revelation 3:20)—and remember, evil spirits are afraid of Jesus! So if you have Jesus in you, and the Holy Spirit in you, you are protected!

- "You, dear children, are from God and have overcome them [evil spirits], because the one who is in you is greater than the one who is in the world" (1 John 4:4).

- Jesus promised, "Peace I leave with you; my peace I give you. I do not give to you as the world gives. Do not let your hearts be troubled and do not be afraid" (John 14:27).

- "You believe that there is one God. Good! Even the demons believe that—and shudder" (James 2:19). See, the demons are afraid of God!

- "Be strong and courageous. Do not be afraid or terrified because of them, for the Lord your God goes with you; he will never leave you nor forsake you" (Deuteronomy 31:6).

As you encourage your children to do these things, you will prepare them to go into their culture and even engage their culture without disobeying God. Deuteronomy 18 clearly forbids God's people from "learning to imitate," "practicing," "engaging in," or "listening to" those who practice sorcery or divination. Remember, God gave these dictates because his people were getting ready to go into a pagan culture. They were to be "in the world" without living as the pagan world lived. There is a significant difference between listening to occult practitioners and hearing about them. To listen to those who practice sorcery would be like reading your horoscope or calling a psychic hotline to hear what they have to say to you. It implies belief in the practice and looking to a source other than God for knowledge. That is forbidden, but it's different from hearing or knowing about such practices. Make this distinction clear.

Teach Them the Truth About Spiritual Realities

Make sure you *personally* have taught each of your children basic Bible truths about the invisible spiritual realm. You can use the explanations offered in chapter 7 as a guideline. If you've witnessed activity in which the kingdom of God has confronted the kingdom of darkness, talk to your kids about these things. For example, as a new Christian and a teen, I attended a Renaissance Fair with some other Christians. We sat in a field to eat lunch about a stone's throw from a row of tents used by fortune-tellers. Before eating, we asked God's blessing on our meal and rather routinely prayed that God would interrupt any forces of evil at work in the tents nearby. Before we could take our first bite, a brightly clad woman burst through the tent panels, bellowing, "Who disturbed my aura?" We were stunned to realize our prayer in Jesus' name had had an immediate effect in the unseen spirit world. The fortune-teller shooed us away, but the lesson I learned that day has remained. I use what happened to illustrate spiritual truth to my kids.

Present your children with a compelling picture of a powerful God who loves them and wants what is best for them. Present "the evil one" (Satan, the devil) as an evil being—murderous, deceitful, and tricky—who was kicked out of heaven for his rebellion against God. Now he is out to destroy those made in the image of God. But God sent Jesus to defeat the works of the devil. Jesus came to give people life in the fullest measure of all that is good. The devil comes to kill, steal, and destroy.

Tell them Bible stories where there is a showdown between the forces of God and the forces of evil—Elijah v. the prophets of Baal (1 Kings 18:16-40), Jesus v. Satan (Matthew 4:1-11), Moses and Aaron v. Pharaoh's magicians (Exodus 7:8-13). Kids will always want to be on the winning side in a battle between good and evil. Other stories, too, can be used to illustrate the true battle between good and evil in the real world. For example, in *The Little Mermaid* the evil one is like Ursula, who tries to trick and destroy

Ariel to get back at her father, King Triton. King Triton is a loving father who gives all to protect and redeem the child he loves from the clutches of the evil one; just as our heavenly Father has given his best to protect and redeem us. In the Harry Potter stories, you can relate the murderous Voldemort, who is out to kill Harry using deception and cunning schemes, to the evil one, Satan. They will figure out for themselves that they don't want to do anything that would leave them vulnerable to that kind of evil character.

Distinguish Between "Magic" in the Fantasy Genre and in Real-Life Settings

I have made a point of teaching our children to differentiate between literary "magic" in a fantasy world and stories in which witchcraft is used in real-life, present-day situations (see chapter 3). I've pointed out that fantasy stories are set apart from our ordinary world. Most kids realize this, but point it out to make sure they don't mistakenly think you're endorsing occult magic. When the setting's real and supernatural powers are used in everyday situations, children are more likely to try what they've seen. Two junior high girls we know tried spells to get rid of acne, then entertained thoughts of calling down curses on their enemies, wrote down harmful messages, and ended up getting expelled from school. All that started with them imitating characters they'd seen in a made-for-television movie.

Clarify that Bible miracles—while truly fantastic—are not fiction. These miracles really happened to real people. While the miracles of the Bible may seem like fiction, these really happened by the supernatural power of God. In contrast, fictional magic is just pretend. You might say something like, "Authors sometimes use magical powers in a story to make it more exciting. It lets them do things beyond what we can do in real life."

My husband and I don't let our kids play any fantasy games in which they participate in reenactment or role-play that involves calling up spirits or anything occult. To help Haley and Taylor understand why, we used a story from the Chronicles of Narnia to illustrate. In *The Last Battle,* there's an "idol" named Tash. Some foolish leaders—who don't really believe Tash exists—pretend to believe in him and call on his name. They're horrified when the real Tash shows up, with disastrous results.

Cultivate and Fortify Your Child's Conscience

Kids need to learn the rules and lists of things that are forbidden by God, but they also need to learn to listen to the Holy Spirit and their own consciences. Kids should be taught that their conscience is the internal alarm system that God gives them to help keep them safe. When their conscience is troubled, they should not dismiss it, but rather should obey it. Let them know that if they continually override their conscience, it will become dull and will no longer be useful to protect them. Help your children listen to the Holy Spirit as he speaks to their conscience about questionable areas. Our son Taylor recently came home from a friend's house and told me how he'd declined playing what his friend called a "super-cool" video game because it was questionable to him.

Our practice of previewing things with Taylor helped instill in him his own criteria for what was unacceptable. Reviewing materials *with* him and helping him exercise critical thinking skills also helped. Once your children understand the basic biblical truths about the occult, test their discernment skills as you encounter the occult in culture. When the witch shows Dorothy her Auntie Em in the crystal ball in *The Wizard of Oz,* ask questions such as: Do you think it is okay to use a crystal ball like that? Why not? Beyond just disobeying God, what are other dangers? The man who told Dorothy what he saw in the crystal ball didn't really see anything. He summed up the situation and used that device as a way of getting Dorothy to go home, suggesting that Auntie Em was sick. He manipulated her for her good. What about those who use such devices to manipulate people to their harm?

Whenever you can, use fictional situations and stories as object lessons.

Wouldn't you prefer these come at the expense of the fictional character rather than your child? When a character has to make a moral decision, use the scenario to help your children think through options and make the best choice. If the character makes a wrong choice and suffers consequences or makes a right choice and is rewarded, use the event as a virtual learning experience. The benefit is that your child is spared the real danger while you help him or her evaluate characters' decisions against the measuring stick of God's Word. Such practice reinforces children's biblical understanding while building moral strength.

Pray, and Teach Your Kids to Pray Effectively!

When our kids tell us about other children having an intense fascination with anything dark, we don't just tell them what's wrong with their friend's behavior, we pray: "God, this kid seems to be under the influence of the evil one. In Jesus' name we ask you to break through any such forces. Protect him from the powerful grip of any evil spiritual forces in his life." Then we let our kids take turns praying. This way, they learn while practicing spiritual warfare.

Seeing results is the best teacher! Our kids consistently remember other kids they want to pray for, especially those who seem to be under the influence of the evil one. Our daughter Casey has been praying for a particular girl at her high school for the past two years. This girl became burdened by her sins and sought out Casey so she could talk about her struggles. She began to hunger to know more about God and even started coming to church. Her appearance and demeanor have changed dramatically as our family has joined Casey in praying for her.

Be Aware of Your Child's Individual Susceptibility to the Occult

Every person has areas of susceptibility that he or she must be aware of and guard against. The Harry Potter books could be more spiritually dangerous for some people than others, especially if one has an unhealthy fascination with occult practices in our world. Consider this analogy[1]: There is nothing particularly evil about a street that has a convenience store, a hotel with a bar in its restaurant, and a donut shop. There is no general rule that prohibits Christians from walking down that street. However, a Christian who has a weakness in an area of lust might see the convenience store and immediately think of the magazine rack stocked with inappropriate magazines. Other Christians might find temptation lurking in the bar or the convenience store cooler where the alcohol is kept. Another Christian with a weakness in the area of gluttony might never give a second thought to the bar but be drawn to the candy racks or the donut shop. God would not give all Christians a general prohibition against going down that street because it could be spiritually dangerous for us or lead us to sin. Rather, the Holy Spirit works in our hearts to let us know where each of us must draw the line in sensitivity to our own areas of susceptibility. It would make sense that these individuals may be advised not to go down that street alone—or perhaps at all. That's why it's good that we have the Holy Spirit with each of us!

If you see that a child is developing an interest in the occult because of references in Harry Potter or any story, wisdom dictates you should avoid that area of susceptibility. Seek the Lord to deal with what is going on in that child's heart and mind.

Every Christian parent, grandparent, and caring adult should prayerfully and carefully consider how the kids we care about are being influenced by popular culture. Pay attention. Ask your children how they think the occult might be influencing their friends. Ask about new fads, what kids are saying, what they believe—and listen. Keep asking questions that lead your kids to figure out good and evil for themselves, to think through where they draw the line with regard to spiritual dangers and things related to the occult. When you listen to your kids, you'll be able to lovingly correct their misconceptions. The least we can do is to read and view anything questionable before allowing them to take it into their hearts and minds. If our consciences are clear, we can take an active role in framing popular culture within biblical truth. Then, instead of just giving them the nod, read or view the material *with them,* teaching them to discern between good and evil in the process. In so doing we can fulfill our spiritual duties and the scriptural admonition that we not be overcome by evil, but overcome evil with good.

CHAPTER NINE

HARRY POTTER AND THE JUDEO-CHRISTIAN ETHIC

Do Rowling's Books Really Promote Secularism and Worldly Values?

"What Shall We Do With Harry?" an article written for Focus on the Family's *Plugged In* magazine, raises a criticism that must be addressed—especially when trying to make good use of the Harry Potter stories for moral instruction. The author, Lindy Beam, presents a balanced weighing of the pros and cons of reading the Harry Potter books. However, she also takes up a common complaint that "Harry frequently—and unapologetically—lies, breaks rules and disobeys authority figures,"[1] and concludes that the Harry Potter stories promote "worldly values." She writes (emphasis mine):

> This is perhaps the most subtle of the dangers in these books, but not one to be overlooked. Since Rowling doesn't make a clear link between her kind of magic and true witchcraft, the spiritual fault of *Harry Potter* is not so much that it plays to dark supernatural powers, but that it doesn't acknowledge any supernatural powers or moral authority at all. *Rowling does not write from the basis of Judeo-Christian ethics.* So her characters may do "the-wrong-thing-for-the-right-reason," often lying, cheating, or breaking rules in order to save the day."[2]

I have read everything I can find written in the Christian community on the subject of Harry Potter. I find Lindy Beam one of the most credible analysts. I sense that her heart is focused on grappling with these complex issues for the good of the body of Christ. She has earned my respect as a writer and a sincere Christian. It also appears that her inclusion of this caution comes from being attentive to comments parents have brought up as reasons they choose not to read the books to their children. Ken McCormick of Birchrunville, Pennsylvania, whose children are eight and eleven, is quoted in *USA Today* as describing "a general nastiness underneath the mantle of cuteness." He says, "The kids lie, they steal, they take revenge. This is a disturbing moral world, and it conflicts with what I am trying to teach my children."[3]

I can see the point of this objection—if one is looking for one-dimensional caricatures of right and wrong behavior. But is that really what older kids need to train them in right living? Sure, that's the way it works on *Sesame Street:* Big Bird is always nice. Oscar the Grouch is always surly. Telly is always nervous. The Count is always—well, counting. So, too, in the genre of melodramas where the villain is dressed in black and only does evil, the hero wears white and does no wrong, and there is no thought given to motives. However, such simplistic moral instruction only goes so far—to about the age of four. Such characters lose their interest to older kids, and they hold no instructive value in a complex moral world. Older kids already know right and wrong; what they have to grapple with is *how* to do right as they grow up in the face of peer pressure.

Granted, Harry Potter is not a simple morality play, but neither is the life of grade-school kids. I propose that the Harry Potter books are deeply moral and can be highly instructive as "training in righteousness" if one rightly aligns these stories to Scripture. The challenge is being sure to make a proper alignment between the elements in the stories and basic elements of Judeo-Christian moral training.

Some will say there is no way to do this because to do so is to try to make witchcraft a good thing. Those who associate the literary magic in Harry Potter with the real occult world need read no further. There is no way to reconcile that objection, and according to Romans 14:23, it would be sinful for a person who has been led by the Lord to assign such meaning to the magical elements to compromise that position. However, those readers who do not make such an association can proceed to see whether Harry Potter's world can be aligned with the Bible in a morally instructive way.

THE HIGHER PRINCIPLES OF THE LAW

First, however, I must contest the conclusion that doing "the-wrong-thing-for-the-right-reason" is clearly outside the Judeo-Christian ethic. I don't do so just to make a point, but rather to demonstrate how you can use the Harry Potter books as redemptive analogies useful for moral instruction. Bear with me for a moment: The criticism of "worldly values" and "secularism" does not hold up because the same criteria would deem Bible examples—both Old Testament (Judeo) and New Testament (Christian)—as being worldly and/or secular. Such criteria would also judge Jesus Christ and the Old Testament hero David as acting contrary to Judeo-Christian ethics. We know that cannot be true, since you don't get more Jewish than David or more Christian than Christ himself.

Let me explain. The gospel of Mark 2:23-28 reads, "Onc Sabbath Jesus was going through the grainfields, and as his disciples walked along, they began to pick some heads of grain. The Pharisees said to him, 'Look, why are they doing what is unlawful on the Sabbath?' [Notice that Jesus doesn't argue that it is not unlawful. It is.]

"He answered, 'Have you never read what David did when he and his companions were hungry and in need? In the days of Abiathar the high priest, he entered the house of God and ate the consecrated bread, which is lawful only for priests to eat. And he also gave some to his companions.'

"Then he said to them, 'The Sabbath was made for man, not man for the Sabbath. So the Son of Man is Lord even of the Sabbath.'"

The incident the Lord Jesus refers to was when David was being hunted down by King Saul. Saul's son Jonathan had warned David that Saul was determined to kill him. So David fled. First Samuel 21 tells the story:

> David went to Nob, to Ahimelech the priest. Ahimelech trembled when he met him, and asked, "Why are you alone? Why is no one with you?"
>
> David answered Ahimelech the priest, "The king charged me with a certain matter and said to me, 'No one is to know anything about your mission and your instructions.' As for my men, I have told them to meet me at a certain place." (verses 1-2)

This is a deliberate lie. The king had not sent David on a mission, but Ahimelech believed him. In verse three David continues,

> "Now then, what do you have on hand? Give me five loaves of bread, or whatever you can find."
>
> But the priest answered David, "I don't have any ordinary bread on hand; however, there is some consecrated bread here—provided the men have kept themselves from women."
>
> David replied, "Indeed women have been kept from us, as usual whenever I set out. The men's things are holy even on missions that are not holy. How much more so today!" So the priest gave him the consecrated bread, since there was no bread there except the bread of the Presence that had been removed from before the LORD and replaced by hot bread on the day it was taken away. (verses 3-6)

Scholars note, "The relationship between the OT incident and the apparent infringement of the Sabbath by the disciples lies in the fact that on both occasions godly men did something forbidden. Since, however, it is always 'lawful' to do good and to save life (even on the Sabbath), both David and the disciples were within the spirit of the law (see Isa 58:6-7; Lk 6:6-11; 13:10-17; 14:1-6)."[4]

Jesus uses the Old Testament account of David's deception and eating the bread Jesus himself acknowledged "was not lawful" to eat to illustrate the principle that it is always lawful to do good and to save life (see Luke 6:9). Such compassionate acts are within the true spirit of the law.[5]

Therefore, we see Jesus Christ himself teaching us that he condoned a time when David (a pillar of Old Testament Judaism) lied, disobeyed the king's orders, and broke a God-given law. And yet, Jesus Christ himself used this example to defend his disciples as they ate grain on the Sabbath when the legalists of his day brought accusations against them. Jesus' disciples were not dying of hunger or even risking death like David was, and yet Jesus condoned their lawbreaking. He did so on the basis of a higher principle in keeping with the spirit of the law.

This is precisely the kind of complex moral decision making found in the Harry Potter books. We see it applied at the playground level in *Harry Potter and the Sorcerer's Stone* when Harry's class is getting ready to take their first broom-flying class. The bully, Draco Malfoy, has been picking on a weaker kid, Neville Longbottom, trying to steal Neville's Remembrall (a small ball that glows to remind you if you've forgotten something). The Remembrall was a gift from Neville's grandmother. In the course of events, Neville falls from his broom, and the teacher tells everyone to stay on the ground until she gets back from taking him to the hospital. When the teacher leaves, Draco takes the Remembrall and flies off, intending to hide it in a tree where Neville can't get it. Harry flies after him to retrieve it, even though Hermione (who's big on following rules) warns him, "Madam Hooch told us not to move—you'll get us all into trouble."[6]

Is this a case of kids learning that it's okay to break rules? Harry is caught going after Neville's Remembrall by Professor McGonogall. She recognizes his talent for flying and catching a small ball in midair, a skill that makes him a natural for the position of Seeker on their house Quidditch team. Professor McGonogall introduces him to the team captain and promises to speak to Professor Dumbledore to see if they can "bend the rule" that says first-year students can't be on the house team. So instead of being punished, Harry is rewarded.

You will note that Professor McGonogall is consistently on the good side and is known for fairness and enforcing rules. She does not favor students in her house, Gryffindor. She docks them points for breaking rules, even when it hurts their common goal to win the House Cup. So it doesn't make sense that she would break rules for the sake of partisan gain. What can be seen here is that she understands the context in which Harry made his decision to break a rule; therefore, she did not hold Harry to the letter of the law. Harry risked punishment for rule breaking—as did Jesus' disciples when they were picking and eating grain on the Sabbath—but it was done in keeping with a higher principle. Harry clearly broke this rule to protect the property of a weaker kid from a bully.

If we think it through, I believe we would agree that there are times on the playground when we don't just want our children to follow the rules, even though the rules are good—so far as they go.

Principles are the overarching purposes and aims that help people determine conduct when there is no specific rule in effect. Right principles are in keeping with the nature of good as revealed in Scripture. What we call the Golden Rule is actually a principle: Do unto others what you would have others do to you, or love your neighbor as yourself. This principle flows from and is in keeping with God's nature of love. So people can figure out what to do in any given situation by remembering this principle and practicing its application.

Rules are devised to apply the general principles of good conduct in specific situations. Some good rules we teach children include keeping your hands to yourself and not hitting people. However, if your son saw three bullies beating up his little sister, he might override the rule "Keep your hands to yourself" to defend her. If, while trying to protect her, it became necessary (to halt deadly violence), he might break the rule "Don't hit."

Isn't this the kind of principled moral decision making we want to train our kids to practice? We can use dependably drawn moral dilemmas to help our kids think it through. In this case, using Harry Potter, we could ask, *Was it right or wrong for Harry to disobey the teacher's rule? Why or why not? Should he have been punished? Are there ever times it's right to break a rule? Since Professor McGonogall was known to uphold the rules, how could she be fair and still not punish Harry for breaking a rule that time?*

The only way children can answer these kinds of questions and make decisions rightly is to understand the *depth* of Judeo-Christian moral training that goes beyond the technicalities of following the law, to the intentions of the lawgiver to do good, preserve life, and protect the weak from those who would oppress them.

Look at how Jesus chided the "rule keepers" of his day, a strict religious sect called the Pharisees. Jesus said, "Woe to you, teachers of the law and Pharisees, you hypocrites! You give a tenth of your spices—mint, dill and cumin. But you have neglected the more important matters of the law—justice, mercy and faithfulness. You should have practiced the latter, without neglecting the former. You blind guides! You strain out a gnat but swallow a camel" (Matthew 23:23-24).

Therefore, *principles* of justice, mercy, and faithfulness are *more important* and *take precedence* over lesser rules whenever the two conflict. Jesus doesn't say we should throw out the lesser rules. Please understand, *I am not excusing disobedience or acting as a rule unto oneself* just because the Harry Potter stories are so engaging. I am not making an argument in favor of giving license for lying, cheating, or covering up wrongdoing to get oneself out of trouble. My point is that we need to teach kids to follow rules in the context of good, unchanging moral principles. As I carefully read the first four Harry Potter books with this moral framework in mind, I found that they hold to the "spirit of the law" in a biblical context.

J. K. Rowling has created a body of literature that is consistently moral within the moral world she created. Kids are eager to read about it. And—whether by design, the influence of her literary training, or an undisclosed spiritual training—the moral world of Harry Potter is in keeping with what the Bible reveals about the nature of good and evil. Therefore, we can *use* these stories for godly purposes—regardless of whether the author intended them to be used for training in Judeo-Christian faith and practice.

HOW CAN WE USE STORIES WHERE HEROES LIE, CHEAT, AND STEAL?

Some suggest the Harry Potter stories are unsuitable for moral training because the lead characters struggle within themselves and don't always do the right thing. They conclude this makes them bad role models, suggesting characters who always do right would be better.

But do we really want to prohibit stories in which the heroes sometimes lie, cheat, or steal? What would that do to our reading of the Bible? Noah got drunk. Abraham lied, "She is my sister." Isaac lied, "She is my sister." Jacob and his mother, Rebecca, conspired to deceive Isaac by devising an elaborate disguise and lying to cover their deception. "Who is there?" asked Isaac. "It is I, your son Esau," said Jacob. "Bless me, Father." Rachel stole her father's household idol, hid it, and lied about it when he came to search, saying, "I can't get up, Father, the way of women is upon me." Ten of the

Patriarchs sold their brother into slavery—a real temptation for some kids!—then lied throughout their lives. They stole Joseph's coat, dipped it in blood to feign his death and cover their treachery, and took it to their distraught father, asking, "Is this the coat of your son, Joseph?" What of Rahab, the prostitute of Jericho, who hid the Israeli spies and lied to those searching for them? She was *rewarded* by God with her life and the lives of her family. Not only that, she also became one of four women mentioned in the lineage of Jesus Christ in Matthew 1!

And it's not just Old Testament saints: What of Peter, who denied that he knew Christ? "I swear to you, I never knew the man!" The list goes on. Just about the only Bible characters whose sins are not revealed are Enoch and Daniel (Daniel only if you don't consider it a problem that he was "chief of the magicians," see chapter 8). The message of the Bible is not about looking for characters who do everything right. There is only one sinless character in the Bible—Jesus, who died for the rest of us! If we decide that we will only read stories to kids where those on the good side never do wrong, we would not be able to read the Bible. Besides, watching characters who battle against evil within themselves and gain mastery over it encourages readers to resist the evil they find within themselves and in their world.

MORAL TRAINING FOR THE PLAYGROUND AND THE BIG, BAD, WORLD

A clear moral understanding of the battle between good and evil is important whether dealing with small-scale playground skirmishes in our world or while chasing a bully on a broomstick in Harry's. However, these childhood lessons are necessary to train children to become good citizens who will—when necessary—fight expressions of evil on a larger scale. We see this over and over in the Harry Potter series as Harry and his friends advance from dealing with the school bully to facing down their world's ultimate evil character, Voldemort. Let me give you an example. (I confess to leaving out some details so as not to give the story away for those who haven't read it!)

In *Harry Potter and the Chamber of Secrets,* a mysterious monster is attacking and "petrifying" Hogwarts students, specifically targeting mudbloods (those who are not of purely magical heritage). Harry's friend Hermione is a mudblood (having Muggle parents, both dentists). She has been "petrified," and Harry and Ron are left to discover what the beast is and how to combat it. In this quest against the forces of evil, they must sneak around the school and misrepresent their true purpose so as not to be stopped. Adding to their difficulty is the reality that not all the adults are on the good side. Thus, unaided by adults, Harry and Ron discover that the fearsome beast is a Basilisk, or King of Serpents, with a murderous stare and venomous fangs. They also learn that its intention is not just to petrify, but to kill.

Harry's and Ron's good intentions are clearly spelled out by the author, although they have to go places students are not allowed and overhear conversations not meant for their ears. Thus they learn the monster has dragged a girl down into the hidden Chamber of Secrets and vows to kill her. It's not just any girl, but someone very dear to them. Ron and Harry want to go to Headmaster Dumbledore for help, but he has been removed from the school over false accusations that he could not keep the students safe from the mysterious attacks.

So Harry and Ron set out to save lives and right many wrongs. In the process, they have to break several rules (such as not being allowed in the corridors without an escort and staying out of the girl's bathroom). They try to get help from a teacher (whose job it is to fight the Dark Arts) but find out he's a self-serving fraud, a coward who is about to run away to protect himself while leaving the girl in danger of certain death. So they disarm the teacher and take him hostage—definitely against the rules—but this is necessary because he is determined to stop their efforts to rescue the girl. Thus they risk their own lives on their way to a showdown with the evil Voldemort.

This is an instance in which the fantasy genre becomes useful to teach about the battle against evil in the larger world—*where it is imperative that children grow beyond the simplistic morality of just minding the rules.* There is a marked parallel between themes in the Harry Potter novels and the kind of horrors our world witnessed under the Nazi regime in World War II. In Rowling's parallel world, Slytherins have a history of murderous hatred toward those of "impure" blood. Twentieth-century history revealed that many churchgoing, rule-keeping people sat idle while atrocities were committed and refused to fight evil because they would have broken the law to do so. They disregarded the greater moral principle of protecting life, preserving justice, and fighting against evil at all costs to stay safely within the letter of the law.

When World War II was over, the extent of the evil was exposed for the world to see and ponder. Both those who participated and those who passively let such horrors happen without resisting evil tried to exonerate themselves by claiming that they were only obeying authority and following orders—keeping the rules. The world rejected these claims and concurred with the true basis of Judeo-Christian ethics, rightfully calling such so-called "morality" immoral. The lesson was clear: When evil is on the march, a higher law supersedes the lesser laws, orders, and rules. When good must fight against evil, we must take to heart what Jesus said to his disciples before they went out into the world, "I am sending you out like sheep among wolves. Therefore be as shrewd as snakes and as innocent as doves" (Matthew 10:16).

It has been said that "The world is not such a bad place because there are so many evil people, but because good people do nothing." If we want our children to take their place in society as moral and courageous citizens who will not sit idly by and let evil overpower good, they must be trained to make principled, moral decisions. This is not secularism or worldly values, it is the epitome of the Judeo-Christian ethic! The Harry Potter books give many examples where this kind of moral courage and principled decision making are in operation. We can use them to train our children to take the side of good against evil, but only if we align the redemptive analogy properly with the Bible.

ALIGNING HARRY POTTER'S WORLD
WITH BIBLICAL MORAL TRAINING

When lining up a spiritual analogy using the Harry Potter books, you start with the basic association that Gryffindor House is on the side of good, while Slytherin House is prone to evil (although not every student in that house is given over to evil). We Christians can associate the symbol of a Lion for Gryffindor House with the biblical symbol of Jesus (supremely good) being the "Lion of the tribe of Judah."[7] We can associate the snake of Slytherin House with the biblical symbol of the evil one represented as a serpent. The first time Satan is introduced in the book of Genesis it is as a serpent who can speak. This carries through to the last book of the Bible where it says, "The great dragon was hurled down—that ancient serpent called the devil, or Satan, who leads the whole world astray. He was hurled to the earth, and his angels with him" (Revelation 12:9). This symbolism holds up as consistent with Rowling's books.

However, we must remain absolutely clear on this point: The author of Harry Potter *never* makes any association between Harry Potter's fantasy world and Satan, the devil, or any other aspect of occult spiritual forces revealed in the Bible as real in our spiritual world. If we *choose* to create such an association, it is our own choice. We can do this successfully because J. K. Rowling has created a moral world that is consistent with the biblical revelation of the nature of good and evil. Therefore, it does not promote secularism or worldly values; rather, it can be used to train children in a higher level of moral discernment based on a deeper understanding of spiritual truth.

Given this understanding, the Harry Potter books can be aligned at viable connecting points with the Bible in a way that can be spiritually and morally useful. Harry and his friends grow in goodness and develop virtues within the community of Gryffindor, with the support of good families like the Weasleys, and under the wise, benevolent leadership of Albus Dumbledore and Professor McGonogall.

There certainly are times when Harry and his friends lie, cheat, deceive, and break rules for no good reason. They cover up something they've chosen to do because they selfishly wanted to do it. There are also times when we get a glimpse into the intensity of their emotions when they are overpowered with feelings they "should not" feel: unabashed hatred, murderous rage, jealousy toward a friend, and vengeance.

In these cases, there is no justification for wrongdoing. Surely we can't use them as good role models when they are clearly doing wrong for wrong reasons to accomplish selfish aims. What is telling in the moral economy of the Harry Potter stories is that there is a marked distinction between those in Gryffindor and those in Slytherin in terms of how they view these episodes.

Those who are seeking to grow in goodness consistently feel guilt and remorse, are forced to acknowledge how their wrongdoing impacts others, and show signs of true empathy and compassion toward those who are hurt by their wrongs. When they do wrong for no good reason, Rowling makes sure they get caught, pay consequences, and are disciplined or instructed. The result is that the reader can watch them growing in goodness under the careful direction of their adult mentors who are on the side of good, seeking to teach and encourage them to defend themselves against the Dark Arts.

We can especially see this kind of moral growth and increasing restraint of selfish human nature taking place in Harry. At the beginning of book three, *Harry Potter and the Prisoner of Azkaban,* Harry's anger is unrestrained when Aunt Marge speaks terribly of his dead parents. He reacts by using magic to inflate her like a balloon (much like the little girl who turned into a blueberry in Roald Dahl's *Charlie and the Chocolate Factory*). Harry lost control of himself and did something he knew was wrong. He got himself into further trouble and extreme danger by running away. He experiences deep remorse and expectation of punishment, which he believes he deserves. Later in that same book, when Professor Snape demeans his dead father, Harry loses his temper and tells him to shut up, but he does not resort to a physical outburst of anger as he did before. Then, toward the end of that same story, we see that Harry has learned to control himself better. When he gets a chance to exact vengeance on someone he believes betrayed his parents to Voldemort and caused their deaths, he does not. At first Ron and Hermione restrain him. But then he restrains himself and chooses not to take revenge when he has the chance. Later he is greatly relieved that he didn't. However, when the one who really betrayed his parents is revealed, Harry has the chance to stand by while others take vengeance. Even so, Harry stops those who are poised to kill the betrayer, saying, "I'm doing it because—I don't reckon my dad would've wanted them to become killers—just for you."[8] So we see Harry's progressive growth in understanding, but also in virtue and self-control.

In contrast to this, those in Slytherin who practice the Dark Arts and follow Voldemort show no signs of conscience. They intentionally foul the Gryffindor team without remorse. They disguise themselves as dementors in an attempt to hurt—and possibly kill—Harry. They have no compassion or empathy for others. They do wrong and enjoy it. They deceive without pangs of conscience. Within that peer group is no positive peer pressure. Instead they prod each other on to do evil. Even their house overseer, Professor Snape, shows a lack of conscientiousness in his unfair treatment of Harry because of the grudge he carries against Harry's dead father. Snape is not purely evil, but he does not offer the students in Slytherin the kind of consistent goodness and principled instruction that Professor McGonogall offers her students in Gryffindor House.

What makes these books useful for helping kids grow in goodness is the alignment with biblical truth. It helps tremendously that the characters are true to life. They are adeptly drawn as real people who must grapple with the frailty of human nature that leaves them prone to do wrong and with hearts that seem inclined toward hatred, envy, vengeance, and other less-than-virtuous traits. And yet those on the side of good persist in seeking truth, justice, and to grow in goodness.

If one is looking for a simple message of "Don't break the rules!" forget the Harry Potter books. But if one is looking for deeper lessons in moral decision making based on principles and a growing discernment of good and evil, these books provide a rare opportunity for such instruction—in keeping with the spirit of Judeo-Christian ethics.

CHAPTER TEN

USING HARRY POTTER TO HELP KIDS GROW IN GOODNESS

An Important Scriptural Pattern of Moral Development

Within the pages of the Harry Potter books, I was amazed to find a brilliant gem: a spiritual truth of utmost importance to young people. I might even argue that it is the most significant understanding a teen needs to have in order to stay on the right path during adolescence. Please follow along with me as I lay out this interesting parallel between Harry Potter and related biblical truths.

Moral and educational development of Hogwarts students in the Harry Potter stories take place in a "house" context. It is worth noting the progressive nature of each story's underlying features:

1. Each tale is set in the context of students belonging to a house or "household"…
2. Where moral and educational development take place…
3. Where students have been "chosen" to "belong"…
4. Although we see via Harry that students exercise free will…
5. And where individual gifts, strengths, and abilities are needed by others…
6. In the context of respect for leaders who teach them…
7. And who offer reproof, correction, and training in right living…

8. Leading to a climax where the heroes have to combat the forces of evil.

Allow me to show how Christian moral development and growing in goodness scripturally parallels these elements. If you make a careful study of Ephesians, you will see all eight features working in the same way and in the same progression. The first three chapters of Ephesians establish our secure place in God's family, *in Christ*. The final three chapters instruct us how to live a righteous life. Let's look at the parallels:

1. Christians are assured that we are *in Christ,* adopted into God's family. If we were talking in Harry Potter terms, that would parallel being adopted into the house of the Lion (Gryffindor).

2. Look at all the assurances we are given in the first half of Ephesians: We were *chosen* (accepted, adopted, sealed) to *belong*. Those who have the assurance that they *securely belong* in God's household *are then* instructed how to live and successfully battle the forces of evil.

3. Even though we are chosen by God to belong to his family...

4. There remains the mystery of free will: "Yet to all who received him, to those who believed in his name, he gave the right to become children of God—children born not of natural descent, nor of human decision or a husband's will, but born of God" (John 1:12-13).

5. Ephesians 4 shows that each of us have gifts that are necessary for the building up of the entire body.

6. We see that within this household, we should respect and submit to God-ordained authority, and that those in authority should lead with love. (This can be seen in the respectful and affectionate relationships that develop within Gryffindor between students and teachers, as contrasted with the kinds of leadership and relationships found in Slytherin.)

7. Beginning in Ephesians 4:25 is a laundry list of bad behavior that those who belong in God's household are to shun. The items on this list are pretty much the same kinds of things Professors Dumbledore and McGonogall and other Gryffindor teachers expound while training Gryffindor students.

8. We are finally told in Ephesians 4:24 to put on our new self and in Ephesians 6:11 to "Put on the full armor of God so that you can take your stand against the devil's schemes," which corresponds to Hogwarts' program of training its students to defend themselves and others against the Dark Arts and climactic battles against evil.

Only after acknowledging our place in God's household and our secure acceptance by God can we effectively proceed to "live a life worthy of the calling you have received" (see Ephesians 3:14–4:1). Whether children understand this foundational truth can make the difference in whether they emerge from adolescence still associating themselves with the household of God. Therefore, whatever can help us make this real for them is a blessing! And I have found a clear illustration of this in Harry Potter we can use to help youth realize this vital spiritual truth. Please let me explain.

In the ten years I spent as a youth minister to middle and high school kids, my mission was "to meet kids at their point of need and lead them to maturity in Christ." The key to doing this was not by reiterating behavior they knew to be right or wrong, nor was it just showing them role models of other kids who chose right over wrong. The key to helping kids transition through the tumultuous junior high and high school years into a life of virtuous living had *everything* to do with the same progression laid out in Ephesians and mirrored in Harry Potter's moral development. Kids needed:

1. To be convinced that they were *acceptable to God* and were therefore members of a household of faith,

2. Help finding *their place* in a peer group where moral training was taking place,

3. To be taught that God had chosen them to belong in his family,

4. To exercise their free will to choose Jesus Christ,

5. To find a place for their unique talents and gifts to fit in, and to appreciate that their gifts were needed by others in the youth group,

which resulted in…

6. Their loving respect for adult leaders and mentors,

7. Their willingness to take reproof, correction, and training in righteousness when they got off track or fell into sin,

8. Their ever-increasing ability to fight and win spiritual battles against forces of evil.

I knew these kids were sure to do wrong sometimes, even after they determined in their hearts that they wanted to live on God's side and do good. Therefore, I also had to reassure them of the love and goodness of God, because it is God's kindness that leads us toward repentance (see Romans 2:4). If they did not understand and firmly believe that they securely belonged in God's household, they would be prone to the accusations and condemnation of Satan.

One girl in my group committed a sin she found grievous. She was so overcome by the realization that she had such potential for wrongdoing that she stopped attending the group. She desperately wanted to do good. She was horrified by what she had done but was nearly convinced that there was no hope for her in God's family. Had she kept these fears to herself, we would have lost her, and she most likely would have given herself over to evil—even though she deeply desired to do good.

When word got back to me, I met with her to remind her that she *belonged* to God, because she had become part of God's family when she put her trust in Jesus Christ. I let her know I was not surprised that she had done something wrong, because the Bible says that when humanity fell under the curse of sin, Satan put a little bit of himself in us. We *all* have a sinful nature that wars within us and entices us to do evil (see Galatians 5).

However, the fact that she had such a strong revulsion to her sin confirmed that God's Spirit was in her. Otherwise, she would not have had such a keen remorse over her capacity for wrongdoing. It was not her exemption from the inner battle of good against evil that proved she belonged to God, but the disposition of her heart and conscience when she faced her own sin nature. She dearly wished to belong to God's household, but secretly feared that her inclination to sin meant she belonged to the evil one.

I believe this kind of spiritual crisis is a crossroads where many good kids give up and give in to their sinful nature. If kids get the impression that "good kids" or "real Christians" never do, think, or feel, anything wrong, they may be deceived into believing they don't *belong* in fellowship with those committed to God. They may give up in the fight against evil that we must continually battle in the power of the Holy Spirit. For the way to overcome such inclination to sin is not by repeating the rules or looking to another good role model; it's by walking in the Spirit in full assurance of our acceptance in Christ. "Those who belong to Christ Jesus have crucified the sinful nature with its passions and desires. Since we live by the Spirit, let us keep in step with the Spirit" (Galatians 5:24-25).

This kind of moral crisis is typical during the teen years. Resolving it rightly is essential before kids can grow in virtuous living as they transition from living under the faith of their parents to establishing their own identity in the household of God. If they are persuaded that their wrestling match with sin—which all of us lose sometimes—means they don't belong to God's household, they will give up. They will connect with other kids whom they believe to be like themselves: "bad." This misconception (and deception by the accuser) is tragic.

However, if they understand that even though they are in the household of God they also bear a "strange likeness" to the evil one, they will not be tricked into believing that evidence of a sinful nature means they belong to the house of evil. Instead they will use their faith (that they do belong to "the good house") to acknowledge their sin nature, respond to the working of the Holy Spirit in their lives, take reproof and correction, and ask for help when they are in battle. Instead of being lured to the dark side, they will draw closer to others on God's side, who can help them keep moving in the right direction, hold them accountable, encourage them, and help them along.

Kids must understand that this kind of inner struggle is common to all human beings—Christians included (see Romans 7). Even though they acknowledge this inner struggle between good and evil, that doesn't mean they are out of God's family. It means they are human! They can still grow in goodness. It just means they are not "inevitably good," as Alan Jacobs wrote of Harry (see p. 24). Therefore, they must not give up, but be all the more vigilant in their spiritual battle against evil.

Harry Potter Can Motivate and Encourage Kids to Grow in Goodness

Harry's struggles against evil can provide motivation for kids to grow in goodness. In some cases, Rowling manages to make even kids who see themselves on the bad side *want* to be on the side of good.

Scholastic Publishers hosts a Harry Potter Discussion Chamber on their Web site. The archives post answers to questions posed about Harry Potter. One question asked kids which house they thought they would be sorted into (see chapter 2) and why. One boy thought he fit in with the Slytherins. He saw himself as sneaky, as someone who'd get along with people like Draco Malfoy. But, he said, Harry "seems to make you want to be in the house of Gryffindor." He called them "such a proud and lively group," citing their bravery and courage with admiration.

Even Christian kids from good homes come to points during adolescence when they worry they may really belong in the equivalent of Slytherin rather than Gryffindor. The fact that the Harry Potter stories make kids *want* to be in Gryffindor is more than half the battle.

The One Illustration That's Worth the Price of the Series

If I found no other spiritual illustration in the Harry Potter books, the one that illustrates this singular truth makes everything worthwhile to me! J. K. Rowling brings this truth to life in a way that captures the heart of what I have seen in the lives of kids at spiritual crossroads. When I read it, tears came to my eyes as I thought of all the kids who have to wrestle with such self-doubts but have no one to correct their misconception. Let me share it with you in hopes that you can use it to explain this important truth for the kids you care about as well.

Throughout the series, the character of Harry Potter is shown to be a good but real boy. He knows the reputation of Slytherin house: Many wizards who graduated from there eventually crossed over to the side of evil. He knows the reputation of Gryffindor house as well: It is devoted to fighting against the Dark Arts and has a rich heritage of noble wizards devoted to the fight against evil. Harry wants to be a Gryffindor!

When Harry arrives at Hogwarts for the first time, he hopes to be sorted into Gryffindor. When the Sorting Hat is set on his head, he hears the hat's voice say, "So, where shall I put you?"

Harry thinks, *Not Slytherin, not Slytherin.*

The hat suggests that Harry could be great in Slytherin, but it heeds Harry's desire and cries out "Gryffindor!" for all to hear.[1] So Harry takes up residence in the house of Gryffindor and becomes part of the fellowship of students in Gryffindor tower.

Later, in book two, Harry and Voldemort confront each other. During the conflict, Voldemort points out to Harry that the two of them have a lot in common: "a strange likeness," including that they are both Parselmouths (able to speak and understand snake language). A battle ensues, but Harry fights bravely and, with help, defeats Voldemort once more.[2]

Sometime after that, Harry explains what happened to him in the Chamber to a group that includes Professor Dumbledore and Professor McGonogall (who points out to Harry that he reached his goal by "breaking a hundred school rules into pieces along the way"). Dumbledore tells Harry how Voldemort became so evil: (1) He sank deeply into the Dark Arts, (2) consorted with the very worst group of wizards, and (3) underwent dangerous magical transformations that dramatically changed him before finally giving himself over to evil. (There's any Christian parent's outline for a three-point sermon!)

Harry is troubled by the possibility that he is a lot like Voldemort and tells Dumbledore what Voldemort said. Dumbledore asks:

"And what do you think, Harry?"

"I don't think I'm like him!" said Harry, more loudly than he'd intended. "I mean, I'm—I'm in *Gryffindor*, I'm…"

But he fell silent, a lurking doubt resurfacing in his mind.

"Professor," he started again after a moment. "The Sorting Hat told me I'd—I'd have done well in Slytherin. Everyone thought *I* was Slytherin's heir for a while…because I can speak Parseltongue…."

"You can speak Parseltongue, Harry," said Dumbledore calmly, "because Lord Voldemort…can speak Parseltongue. Unless I'm much mistaken, he transferred some of his own powers to you the night he gave you that scar. Not something he intended to do, I'm sure…."

"Voldemort put a bit of himself in *me?*" Harry said, thunder-struck.

"It certainly seems so."

"So I *should* be in Slytherin," Harry said, looking desperately into Dumbledore's face. "The Sorting Hat could see Slytherin's power in me, and it—"

"Put you in Gryffindor," said Dumbledore calmly. "Listen to me, Harry. You happen to have many qualities Salazar Slytherin prized in his hand-picked students.... Yet the Sorting Hat placed you in Gryffindor. You know why that was. Think."

"It only put me in Gryffindor," said Harry in a defeated voice, "because I asked not to go in Slytherin...."

"Exactly," said Dumbledore, beaming once more. "Which makes you *very different* from [the one who became Voldemort]. It is our choices, Harry, that show what we truly are, far more than our abilities."[3]

So Harry Potter is a model of a young person on a quest to find out who he truly is and where he truly belongs. He is chosen to be in Gryffindor, and he chooses to be there. He longs to be good while strug-gling with certain traits that seem to have more in common with the evil one than with heroes on the side of good. He must constantly be on guard against an evil adversary, who is deceptive and deadly. Above all, he must resist evil regardless of how weak he feels. He is discovering that he does have courage. He is a Seeker in more ways than one; he seeks truth, and he seeks to right wrongs and overturn injustice. He is not alone, not even when he seems to stand alone in his battle against the evil one. He is humble enough to call out for help and brave enough to make good use of the help he receives. He is in the process of discovering he has some unique talents, but also learning that he cannot get by without the help and unique talents of his friends. He does not know what destiny holds for him, but he knows his heritage, he knows the house where he belongs, and he is determined to resist evil. I don't know how you see it, but that sounds like a pretty good illustration of the Christian life to me.

If we turn our attention from one-dimensional role models who do everything right to complex characters who parallel the real way kids grow in goodness and mature in their commitment to resist evil, we find that the Harry Potter stories are rich in parallels to our Judeo-Christian faith. We have to put some effort into learning to recognize these and correctly handle the word of truth, but it's worth the effort when it helps real kids we love resist evil and grow in goodness.

Chapter Eleven

USING HARRY POTTER TO PREACH THE GOSPEL

Turning Stories into Evangelistic Tools

The Harry Potter debate has taken many turns over the course of the series' history. During the ongoing debate, Focus on the Family has done a great job of pointing out valid concerns, providing book reviews in *Plugged In* magazine, and giving balanced presentations of various positions both pro and con. Lindy Beam, youth culture analyst for Focus on the Family, has made statements both positive and negative toward the series. However, recently she had this to say in "What Shall We Do With Harry?"

> While Christians have good reason to be concerned about *Harry Potter,* something has gone sadly awry in how these concerns have played out. Specifically, I'm troubled by two things: that we're miss-ing a huge opportunity to be salt and light in our world, and that we've taken too simplistic a view of what our reaction must be to the problematic elements of *Harry Potter.*
>
> Clearly the church is not *gaining* any ground over this issue. We may succeed in defending our own homes against the "invasion," but we are not winning unbelieving hearts and minds to Christ.

Harry Potter is popular, in part, because it touches on deep human questions about a reality beyond the physical. Christians have an opportunity to intelligently challenge the dangers we see in *Harry Potter* and give evidence of a better answer found in Christ. But instead of capitalizing on this opportunity, our fear gives us an excuse to be reactionary, remain ignorant or both. If we continue to choose these approaches, the church will remain a small voice shouting from the bleachers rather than a quarterback in the cultural huddle.

Specifically, we've oversimplified what the church's approach to *Harry Potter* should be. We have taken to heart the biblical admonition to "have nothing to do with the fruitless deeds of darkness…," but we have neglected our responsibility to "expose them" (Eph. 5:12). In other words, we've done the reactive part, but we've dismissed the proactive part of what God calls us to do…. I would propose instead that reading *Harry Potter* produces *curiosity* and that it is what we do with that curiosity that makes all the difference.[1]

FRIENDSHIP EVANGELISM

Let me share with you a story of how I was able to use the interest in and curiosity aroused by the Harry Potter books in the way Lindy Beam suggests we should.

Our family had been praying for another family in our neighborhood for several years. Their daughter, Sarah, is a close friend of our children. We made the acquaintance of the parents, Sue and Tullie, during school field trips, where one parent from each of our families always volunteered. Over the years, our children invited Sarah to church. She came to our summer VBS activities and even sang in the Christmas musical. My husband and I were friendly with the girl's parents, but most of our conversations revolved around our children. They knew we were Christians, but we were not sure where they stood with the Lord. We hoped to present the gospel to them clearly, but the opportunity didn't materialize. They came to the church picnic once for a few minutes. They also attended the Christmas musical to watch their daughter perform. But our attempts to turn the conversation to a clear presentation of the gospel didn't go anywhere.

Their daughter was the first person to introduce our family to Harry Potter. Since each of our families enjoyed reading, we would often compare notes on books we thought the other might enjoy. At their recommendation—and because I was concerned about the elements of witchcraft—I read the first book. That's when I saw a way to turn a conversation about Harry Potter into a parable of the saving grace of Jesus Christ and his triumph over Satan.

I'm always looking for ways to connect something in popular culture to some truth from the Bible in an effort to win people to Christ. Scripturally, I see this akin to Paul preaching on Mars Hill (Acts 17:23) and relating the gospel to an inscription he read on one of their many idols. Paul—inspired by the Holy Spirit—sums up my attitude with his words in 1 Corinthians 9:22-23: "I have become all things to all men so that by all possible means I might save some. I do all this for the sake of the gospel." I, too, use cultural connections to relate the gospel. I don't know if this tendency is part of my evangelistic gifting, training as a communicator, or both. Regardless, I thank God for it, because he used it to give me the opportunity we'd been praying for to share Christ with Sarah's father.

The opportunity arose when Tullie mentioned that he had heard a man on Christian talk-radio denouncing the Harry Potter books. He said he didn't understand that point of view; his family loved the books. I explained to him that parents were justifiably concerned that their children could be confused by the occult terminology and be exposed to real occult practices. I told him that I, too, take seriously the need to protect my kids from occult influences. However, I had found an analogy to the love of Jesus

Christ and his power over Satan in *Harry Potter and the Sorcerer's Stone*. He was surprised by this and very intrigued. He wanted to hear how I could present the gospel from Harry's story.

Here is what I told him:

Harry finds out that his parents were murdered by the evil Voldemort. Voldemort tried to kill Harry with the same curse that killed Harry's father and mother. The great mystery is why Harry didn't die. No one else had ever been able to survive the curse of death from Voldemort. But Harry lived! And he was just a baby!

Near the end of the book, it comes out that Voldemort killed Harry's father first. Then he aimed the curse of death at Harry, but the baby's mother, Lily, threw herself in front of the curse to save him. She loved him so much that she laid down her life for him. She took the full force of the curse of death to protect Harry, even though she *didn't have* to die. (This is explained on p. 294 of the first book.) At that moment, Voldemort's power was broken, and he didn't understand why. He tried to kill Harry again, but Harry lived. As soon as Voldemort's power was broken, he went into hiding.

I explained that the evil character Voldemort could be compared to Satan (even though in the story he began as a human wizard who went bad). The Bible says there is a real *evil one* in our world called Satan or the devil. Jesus said, the evil one and his followers come to "steal and kill and destroy; I come that they may have life, and have it to the full." (John 10:10). Voldemort came to steal (the Sorcerer's Stone), to murder (Harry's dad, mom, Harry, and many others), and to destroy. Like Voldemort, Satan is associated with darkness and death. A long time ago, Satan tricked people into rebelling against God. This caused people to fall under the curse of death that God had warned them against. Romans 6:23 says, "For the wages of sin is death."

But God loved the world so much that he came up with a plan to break the curse of death so that people would have the chance to live forever with him. This plan was to send Jesus Christ to Earth. Jesus grew up without ever disobeying God's law. He never sinned, so he never brought the curse of death on himself. Jesus was arrested and crucified by evil men who were doing Satan's dirty work. They thought they could destroy Jesus, but instead of destroying Jesus, the curse of death was destroyed. This parallels how Harry received the gift of life and overcame death when his mother— driven by her love for him—sacrificed her life for his. Likewise, the world received "the gift of God [which] is eternal life in Christ Jesus our Lord" (Romans 6:23) when Jesus sacrificed his life for us.

Lily Potter jumped in front of Voldemort's curse to save Harry; Jesus jumped in front of death's curse to save us. Galatians 3:13 says, "Christ redeemed us from the curse of the law by becoming a curse for us, for it is written: 'Cursed is everyone who is hung on a tree.' " The Bible says, "God so loved the world that he gave his one and only Son, that whoever believes in him shall not perish but have eternal life" (John 3:16). Jesus' friend and follower, John, explained it this way: "This is how God showed his love among us: He sent his one and only Son into the world that we might live through him. This is love: not that we loved God, but that he loved us and sent his Son as an atoning sacrifice for our sins" (1 John 4:9-10).

Voldemort's power was broken when Mrs. Potter willingly sacrificed her life for Harry; Satan's power was broken when Jesus died on the cross to sacrifice his life for us. Jesus did this "so that by his death he might destroy him who holds the power of death—that is, the devil" (see Hebrews 2:14-15). Lily Potter gave her life and took the curse on herself; she died and there was no remedy for her. If Jesus had been a mere human being, he would have had to pay the wages of sin for himself and would not have been able to rise from the dead. However, because Jesus was sinless, Acts 2:24 says, "God raised him from the dead, freeing him from the agony of death, because it was impossible for death to keep its hold on him." It's helpful to remember this connection to Jesus' sacrificial death and resurrection by making the association between Lily Potter's first name and the Easter lily.

Jesus rose from the dead—not as a ghost, but in a resurrected body. This proved that he broke the curse of death that Satan had hanging over the human race. So if we trust in Jesus and what he did on the cross, we don't have to be afraid to die someday. We can be assured of eternal life. The evil one doesn't have the power anymore to use the curse of death against those who trust in Jesus. Whoever believes in Jesus will not perish but will have everlasting life. Even though our bodies will die, we will go on to eternal life, and someday our bodies will be resurrected too.

God wants all of us to be safely in his care and confident of his protection from evil. Jesus promised all who would open their hearts to him that he would come in to their lives (see Revelation 3:20). He said he would never leave us and also promised his disciples that the Holy Spirit would be in them and with them. Acts 2 tells us that the promise of the Holy Spirit is extended to all disciples throughout time. When we have Jesus Christ as our Savior, belong to the family of God, and have the Holy Spirit, we can trust God to keep us safe from the evil one.

Beyond this, God provides protection for his followers from the power of the evil one. This, too, can be associated with the Harry Potter story line. Harry's triumph over death "stumped" Voldemort; he disappeared. He became an (as yet) diminished spirit-being, still at work behind the scenes, trying to destroy Harry. We, too, have a malevolent spiritual enemy working invisibly behind the scenes. We are to remain on alert. First Peter 5:8-9 warns, "Be self-controlled and alert. Your enemy the devil prowls around like a roaring lion looking for someone to devour. Resist him, standing firm in the faith," just as Harry must ever be on alert against the attacks of Voldemort and resist him actively. Jesus taught his followers to include the request that God "deliver us from the evil one" in the Lord's Prayer.

However, God doesn't want us to be afraid. Jesus has authority over the evil one and extends this power to his disciples (see Luke 10:17-20). When we think of how Voldemort's curse could not kill Harry, the lightning bolt scar on Harry's forehead can symbolize that God cast Satan down like lighting. Satan's power is not equal to God's. So while we have to resist the evil one, we don't have to live in fear. We see this in the way Harry and Dumbledore are not afraid to say Voldemort's name.

When we trust God's power and protection, the evil one won't be able to touch us! This idea, too, can be found in the story. Harry and a character who allowed Voldemort to work through him—while keeping it under his hat—have a showdown. Acting under Voldemort's orders, this character tries to put his hands on Harry to kill him. But *he couldn't touch Harry!* He was burned every time he tried. Harry had some kind of invisible protection that made the enemy unable to kill him or even touch him. Professor Dumbledore explained to Harry, "Your mother died to save you. If there is one thing Voldemort cannot understand, it is love. He didn't realize that love as powerful as your mother's for you leaves its own mark. Not a scar, no visible sign…to have been loved so deeply, even though the person who loved us is gone, will give us some protection forever."[2] So we Christians need to be vigilant against evil but also trust that we have been sealed with the protection of the Holy Spirit. God has not given us a spirit of fear, but of love, and power, and a sound mind. Each of us can know that "the one who is in [us] is greater than the one who is in the world [Satan]" (1 John 4:4).

Sarah's father listened intently as I shared the gospel with him in this way, stopping me occasionally to ask for clarification. Afterward, he better understood why some Christians were so concerned about their children reading these books, especially without any biblical instruction or warnings. He also could no longer think of the first Harry Potter book without considering how Jesus Christ had died for him, took the curse of death in his place, rose from the dead, giving us authority over and protection from the real invisible forces of evil in this world.

Sadly, a few months later this family suffered a terrible loss. Sue died suddenly and without warning from undiagnosed lung cancer. In their time of crisis, our family and church reached out to Tullie and ten-year-old Sarah with the love of the Lord. Within a few weeks, Tullie accepted Jesus Christ as his personal Savior and began attending church with our family. Sarah, who—we found out later—had trusted Christ previously through our children's witness to her, joined the kids worship/drama team and was baptized.

That is how our family has been able to preach the gospel using the Harry Potter story. I have also used this approach to present the gospel to several other people, who would not have entered into conversation with me *to discuss Jesus,* but were intrigued enough to go there while discussing our common interest in Harry Potter.

The Importance of Using Stories to Reach This Generation

Last summer I attended DC/LA 2000, a huge youth-evangelism training conference produced by Youth for Christ (YFC). Their approach for reaching this generation of young people came down to a basic formula represented by three interconnected circles. Each circle represented a story: God's story, your story, and their story. "Their story" represents the story of the person with whom you are trying to share the gospel. YFC taught us about the characteristics of this generation of youth and the important role stories play in reaching them. They also stressed how important it is not to focus our attention on just *telling God's story,* but to give at least as much attention to *listening to their stories.* Listening to what matters to them is the connecting point we use to connect God's story about the life, death, and resurrection of Jesus Christ to their story.

This generation of kids have shown us that the Harry Potter stories are important to them. We can use their love of these stories in many ways. We can use them as a point of conversation, as I did with Tullie. We can use them to gain insight into what touches kids' hearts and what they hunger for spiritually and emotionally. If you are interested in doing this, I have a suggestion: Go to the Scholastic.com Web site and read the answers kids give to discussion questions asked about the Harry Potter books. When you read the answers, *listen to the hearts of these kids.* When I did this, I was filled with a rekindled desire to find a way to share the love and power of God with this generation of youth.

If you know kids who love the Harry Potter books, make sure you have cautioned them and educated them about the dangers of occult involvement in our world. But if you want to lead them to Christ, get to know their stories and connect God's story (the gospel) to theirs. Let me show you how to connect with a kid who loves Harry Potter and how to use the story they know and enjoy to lead them to salvation through Jesus Christ.

It's no wonder everyone was seeking the Sorcerer's Stone in the first Harry Potter book. It promised to give the one who had it gold and eternal life. Who wouldn't want that? It seems that everyone in our world wants riches and wants to live forever. God put that desire in our hearts, because there is a place He wants us to go (heaven) where we can walk on streets of gold and live forever with God. But nobody can steal their way in. The only way to get into heaven is to have the curse of sin (that part of us that wants to do wrong, and the punishment wrongdoing deserves) taken away. The punishment for sin is death, but the free gift of God is eternal life through Jesus Christ.

Jesus Christ loved you so much that he took the curse of death for you. He was nailed to a cross, bled, and died to pay for your sins. Three days later he came back to life. This proved he had broken the curse of death. Now whoever believes in him will have everlasting life. Jesus then ascended (floated) up into the sky while his followers watched. He promised he was going away to prepare a place for all who would believe in him and follow him. That place (most people call heaven) is described in Revelation 21:10 through Revelation 22:5. The streets are paved with gold! The walls are covered with priceless jewels! The gates are made of pearls! Best of all—no longer will there be any curse! (Rev. 22:3), and God's servants will rule with him forever and ever. If you want to live forever in heaven with God, here is what you need to do:

1. Believe that Jesus Christ took the curse of death for you when he died on the cross.
2. Receive Jesus as your personal Savior. Say, "Yes, Jesus, I accept your gift" and thank him for it.
3. Seek God with all your heart (with the same kind of enthusiasm and determination Harry and friends showed as they sought the Stone that promised to give immortality and riches).
4. Pray a prayer something like this:

Dear God,

Thank you for sending your only Son, Jesus, to take the curse of death to pay for my sins. Thank you Jesus for dying on the cross to save me. I receive Jesus as my Savior and his gift of eternal life. Thank you for hope of heaven where we will walk on streets of gold. Please forgive all my sins and help me grow in goodness. I want to be someone in your house who does all I can to win in the battle against evil. Help me learn to resist the evil one and to be brave and strong by your power. Amen!

If you want to get to know their hearts, ask them some of the questions being asked in the Harry Potter Discussion Chambers. Don't ask about witchcraft (on that issue we need to inform them), but ask questions like these: What do you think you would see if you looked in the Mirror of

Erised (which reveals a person's unfulfilled desires)? Which house do you think you would be sorted into and why? Which of the characters do you like best or identify with most and why? What shape would a boggart take if it appeared before you (then listen for their greatest fear)?

If you or your child are not confident that you are safely in God's care, call the pastor or children's pastor of your local church. Schedule an appointment so those concerns can be put to rest. This can be a wonderful opportunity to make the reality of salvation clear for your child.

Thanks to these books, you can enter into heart-to-heart conversations with young people. Ask. Then listen to their stories, their unfulfilled desires, their fears. Listen and love. Then find a way to connect God's love story to theirs. Even if you make a conscientious decision not to read or see the Harry Potter stories or allow your children to, prayerfully consider how you could use the popular interest in them to share the love of God with the young people who love Harry Potter.

PUTTING THE HARRY POTTER PHENOMENON TO WORK IN MINISTRY

Leonard Sweet is professor of evangelism at Drew University, where he has served for the last five years as dean of the School of Theology, vice-president, and professor of postmodern Christianity. He holds a master of divinity degree and a Ph.D. He is a noted expert on ministering effectively to this generation. He writes, "The best way to defuse the principalities and powers of postmodern culture is not to escape from it, but to learn its language...and engage it on a higher level."[3]

I believe the Harry Potter stories have become an integrated part of the language of this generation. I pray that all Christians who are not restricted by conscience from reading the books will make sure they don't merely conclude it is *lawful* for them to read Harry Potter, but will go on to make it *profitable* for the body of Christ. Following are some ideas of how the body of Christ in general, and your church in particular, might consider making the Harry Potter phenomenon pay off in ministry.

- Discuss issues of occult influence in culture and make sure that children in your congregation understand how and why to eschew occult involvement.
- Discuss how Christians are to make conscientious decisions in disputable matters.
- Discuss and teach how Christians should treat each other when we disagree about important spiritual issues without disgracing the Lord and hurting each other.
- Discuss and plan ways we Christians can relate to our culture in respectful and effective ways that bring biblical truths into the public forum of ideas.
- Discuss and teach how to be "in the world but not of the world."
- Discuss issues of spiritual warfare, especially the importance of educating and equipping children and adults to overcome evil and resist the devil by putting on spiritual armor, firmly holding the shield of faith, and wielding the Sword of the Spirit.
- Consider how popular literature reveals the heartfelt needs of a generation. Pray, asking God to show us how we can respond to these real needs.
- The Harry Potter movies are coming out. Some may go to "protest and picket." However, consider whether there isn't a better way to meet this opportunity. Perhaps we could develop tracts or other materials that connect the Harry Potter story to the gospel story. Then, instead of condemning those who are interested in Harry Potter, we could use that interest as an open door to share with them the greatest story of all.

"Do not be overcome by evil,
but overcome evil with good" (Romans 12:21).

NOTES

Chapter One

1. Adapted from BreakPoint, November 2, 1999, copyright 1999, reprinted with permission of Prison Fellowship, P.O. Box 17500, Washington, DC, 20041-7500. www.christianity.com/breakpoint.

2. Berit Kjos, "Bewitched by Harry Potter," Kjos Ministries (December 24, 1999). Found at http://www.crossroad.to. Used by permission.

3. John Andrew Murray, "Harry Dilemma," *Teachers in Focus* (February 2000). Found at http://www.family.org/cforum/teachersmag/. Author is headmaster at St. Timothy's-Hale in Raleigh, NC. Used by permission.

4. Lindy Beam, "Exploring Harry Potter's World." From *Focus on the Family* magazine. Vol. 24, No. 5 (May 2000): 15, published by Focus on the Family. Copyright © 2000, Focus on the Family. All rights reserved. International copyright secured. Used by permission.

5. Michael G. Maudlin, "Virtue on a Broomstick," *Christianity Today* (September 4, 2000): 117-9. Author is online executive editor. Used by permission, Christianity Today International, copyright © 2000.

6. Alan Jacobs, "Harry Potter's Magic," *First Things: A Monthly Journal of Religion and Public Life* (January 2000). Found at http://www.firsthings.com/ftissues/ft0001/reviews/jacobs.html. Author is professor of English at Wheaton College.

7. Alison Lentini, "Harry Potter: Occult Cosmology and the Corrupted Imagination...an excerpt," Spiritual Counterfeits Project. Found at http://www.scp-inc.org/publications/journals/J2304/PotterArticle.htm. (This address is case sensitive.) Author was involved in Wicca and neo-paganism before coming to know Christ. She has a BA and MA in romance languages and literatures at Princeton University.

8. *Christianity Today* editorial, "Why We Like Harry Potter," *Christianity Today* (1999). Found at http://www.christianitytoday.com/ct/2000/001/29.37.html.

9. Phill Allen, "Letters to the Editor," *Christianity Today* (December 13, 1999). Found at http://www.christianitytoday.com.

10. Marcia Hoehne, "Letters to the Editor," *Christianity Today* (March 27, 2000). Found at http://www.christianitytoday.com.

11. Andrew Cipiti, "Letters to the Editor," *Christianity Today* (July 28, 2000). Found at http://www.christianitytoday.com.

Chapter Two

1. J. K. Rowling, *Harry Potter and the Sorcerer's Stone* (New York: Scholastic Press, 1998), 1.

2. Rowling, *Sorcerer's Stone*, 57.

3. Rowling, *Sorcerer's Stone*, 118.

4. Rowling, *Sorcerer's Stone*, 118.

5. Rowling, *Sorcerer's Stone*, 118.

6. Rowling, *Sorcerer's Stone*, 118.

Chapter Three

1. J. K. Rowling, as quoted in "Success of Harry Potter bowls author over" (October 21, 1999). Found at http://www.cnn.com/books/news/9910/21/rowling.intvu/index.html.

2. Helen M. Jerome, "Welcome Back, Potter," *Book* (May/June 2000): 43.

3. Thomas L. Martin, ed., *Reading the Classics with C. S. Lewis* (Grand Rapids, Mich.: Baker, 2001), 277.

4. Rowling, *Sorcerer's Stone*, 220.

5. Anthony M. House, "Newton and Flamel on Star Regulus of Antimony and Iron, Part 1," as found through http://www.askjeeves.com by requesting: "Nicolas Flamel," then by clicking "ask" following the prompted question "Where can I learn more about the occult figure Newton and Flamel?"

6. From an interview with J. K. Rowling. Found at http://www.scholastic.com/harrypotter/author/interview.htm., in answer to "Any

hints you could share about what to expect in future Harry Potter books?" (Obtained September 5, 2000).

7. Popularized by psychologists in the 1930s, this drawing is often referred to as the Boring figure (after psychologist E. G. Boring) and has appeared in a variety of forms over the years. This image was first published by cartoonist W. E. Hill in 1915, although the appearance of a similar image on an 1888 German postcard is its earliest known form.

8. C. S. Lewis, "The Genesis of a Medieval Book," as quoted by Walter Hooper, *C. S. Lewis: A Companion and Guide* (HarperSanFrancisco, 1996), 430.

9. Nevill Drury, "Elves" entry in *Dictionary of Mysticism and the Occult* (San Francisco: Harper & Row, 1985), as quoted by Jack Roper, "Harry Potter: The Hero for Modern Witchcraft" (October 27, 2000). Found at http://www.cbn.com.

10. J. K. Rowling, in an interview with Katie Couric on NBC's *Today Show* (October 20, 2000).

Chapter Four

1. Gene Del Vecchio, *Creating Ever-Cool: A Marketer's Guide to a Kid's Heart* (Gretna, La.: Pelican Publishing, 1997), 25.

2. Adapted from BreakPoint, July 14, 2000, copyright 2000, reprinted with permission of Prison Fellowship, P.O. Box 17500, Washington, DC, 20041-7500. www.christianity.com/breakpoint.

3. Del Vecchio, *Creating Ever-Cool,* 178.

4. Del Vecchio, *Creating Ever-Cool,* 71, 73.

5. Del Vecchio, *Creating Ever-Cool,* 73, 81.

6. Rowling, *Sorcerer's Stone,* 213-4.

7. Del Vecchio, *Creating Ever-Cool,* 172-3.

8. Rowling, *Sorcerer's Stone,* 80.

9. Del Vecchio, *Creating Ever-Cool,* 176.

10. Martin Seligman, *The Optimistic Child* (New York: Houghton Mifflin, 1995), 33.

11. Del Vecchio, *Creating Ever-Cool,* 67-8.

12. Paul F. Ford et al., *Companion to Narnia* (HarperSanFrancisco, 1994), 434-5. Text copyright © 1980 by Paul F. Ford. Reprinted by permission of HarperCollins Publishers, Inc.

13. Caller identified only as Peter from Louisiana. *CNN Talkback Live* (July 7, 2000). Found at http://www.cnn.com.

14. As quoted in Del Vecchio, *Creating Ever-Cool,* 70.

15. Rowling, *Sorcerer's Stone,* 34.

Chapter Five

1. Kenneth Barker, ed., notes for 1 Cor. 10:14, *The NIV Study Bible* (Grand Rapids, Mich.: Zondervan, 1985), 1747.

2. Lindy Beam wrote: "Children who read about Harry Potter will probably discover little to nothing about the true world of the occult. That's why some Christian leaders and Christian publications find these books to be more fantastical than threatening." ("What Shall We Do With Harry?" *Plugged In* [July 2000], as seen on http://www.family.org. Copyright © 2000, Focus on the Family. All rights reserved. International copyright secured. Used by permission.) See also Charles Colson's remarks in his *BreakPoint* commentary "Witches and Wizards: The Harry Potter Phenomenon" in chapter 1 of this book.

3. Barker, notes for 1 Cor. 10:20, *NIV Study Bible,* 1748.

Chapter Six

1. Every effort was made to locate and give attribution to the author of this e-mail. Several sources name the author as Roger Lynn; however, this could not be verified. If you can provide knowledge of the authorship of this piece so that he or she may receive proper attribution, please contact the publisher.

2. Bob Liparulo, "Harry Potter: Should you be afraid of this boy?" *New Man* (November/December 2000): 66-7.

3. Beam, "Exploring Harry Potter's World," 15.

4. Rowling, as quoted in "Success of Harry Potter."

5. Bryan Hupperts, "Letters to the Editor," *Christianity Today* (August 2000).

6. Lewis, as quoted in *C. S. Lewis: A Companion and Guide*, 552.

7. C. S. Lewis, *Prince Caspian* (New York: Macmillan, 1970), 189-90.

8. Lewis, *Prince Caspian*, 160.

9. Lewis, *Prince Caspian*, 165.

10. Lewis, *Prince Caspian*, 162-3.

11. Lewis, *Prince Caspian*, 192-3.

12. Lewis, *Prince Caspian*, 83.

13. Ford, *Companion to Narnia*, 285-6.

14. Lewis, *Prince Caspian*, 73.

15. Ford, *Companion to Narnia*, 68.

Chapter Seven

1. Rowling, as quoted in "Success of Harry Potter."

2. W. E. Vine, *An Expository Dictionary of New Testament Words* (Westwood, N.J.: Revell), 1074-5.

Chapter Eight

1. This helpful analogy was suggested to me by Rich Buhler, who at the time of our conversation had not read the Harry Potter books and does not necessarily endorse them.

Chapter Nine

1. John Andrew Murray, "The Trouble with Harry," *Citizen* (2000). Found at http://www.family.org.

2. Beam, "What Shall We Do with Harry?"

3. As quoted by Deirdre Donahue, "Harry Potter madness strikes at midnight" *USA Today* (July 7, 2000). Found at http://www.usatoday.com/life/enter/books/book759.htm.

4. Barker, notes for Mark 2:25, *NIV Study Bible*, 1497.

5. Barker, notes for 1 Samuel 21:4, *NIV Study Bible*, 407.

6. Rowling, *Sorcerer's Stone*, 148.

7. See reference to Jesus being the "Lion of the tribe of Judah" in Revelation 5:5.

8. J. K. Rowling, *Harry Potter and the Prisoner of Azkaban* (New York : Arthur A. Levine Books, 1999), 376.

Chapter Ten

1. Rowling, *Sorcerer's Stone*, 121.

2. J. K. Rowling, *Harry Potter and the Chamber of Secrets* (New York: Scholastic, 1999), 314-26.

3. Rowling, *Chamber of Secrets*, 332-3.

Chapter Eleven

1. Beam, "What Shall We Do with Harry?"

2. Rowling, *Sorcerer's Stone*, 299.

3. Leonard Sweet, *SoulTsunami* (Grand Rapids, Mich.: Zondervan, 1999), 21.

ACKNOWLEDGMENTS

The support and partnership of my husband, Patrick, was an integral part of bringing this book to completion. I relied heavily on his editorial feedback, guidance, and encouragement.

My agent, Sealy Yates, helped me reframe the project after I had laid it aside. I appreciate his energetic representation, which brought this to the right publisher at the right time.

WaterBrook Press has been everything an author could hope for in a publisher! I'm especially grateful for the special attention given this project by publisher Dan Rich and senior editor Erin Healy. My thanks also to the entire WaterBrook team. I now have a new standard for what a *Christian* publishing relationship can be.

Thanks to Paul and Bridgette Robins for giving me a place to seclude myself (and for the homemade soup!) during the formative phase of this work.

I'm grateful to our pastor, Dr. David A. George, for able biblical critique on chapters that required theological review and for his leadership of our church, which was of great support during this project.

Today's Christian Woman magazine and its managing editor, Jane Johnson Struck, gave me the opportunity to address these issues first in the pages of *TCW* (September/October 2000). I appreciate their willingness to take on such a controversial topic.

My thanks to Craig Von Buseck at http://www.CBN.com, who gave me the opportunity to put forth some of this material on their Web site. The Internet exposure allowed me to get immediate feedback from those on both sides of the Harry Potter debate. And the exposure proved highly valuable because it let me listen in on the arguments and take to heart a wide range of personal opinions within the Christian community.

Many people who have given serious thought to the Harry Potter debate helped to shape my views. Everyone who has dared to think through this issue in the light of public scrutiny, with a careful attention to Scripture and genuine concern for the protection of children and the advancement of God's kingdom, has my gratitude.